EMILE FOR TODAY

EMILE FOR TODAY

The *Emile* of
Jean Jacques Rousseau

SELECTED, TRANSLATED AND INTERPRETED

by

WILLIAM BOYD
M.A., B.Sc., D.Phil., D.Litt., LL.D.

HEINEMANN
LONDON

Heinemann Educational Books Ltd
LONDON EDINBURGH MELBOURNE AUCKLAND TORONTO
SINGAPORE HONG KONG KUALA LUMPUR
IBADAN JOHANNESBURG NAIROBI
LUSAKA NEW DELHI

TO
BEATRICE ENSOR
Founder of the New Education Fellowship
in admiring regard

ISBN 0 435 80100 7

FIRST PUBLISHED 1956
REPRINTED 1958, 1960, 1963, 1964, 1966
1968, 1970, 1973
REPRINTED AS A LIMP EDITION 1975

Published by
Heinemann Educational Books Ltd
48 Charles Street, London W1X 8AH
Printed Offset Litho and bound in Great Britain by
Cox & Wyman Ltd, London, Fakenham and Reading

CONTENTS

EDITOR'S PROLOGUE

AMONG the multitude of writings about education in the modern world the *Emile* of Jean Jacques Rousseau is the one which has exercised the greatest influence on the course of educational thought and practice.

Rousseau was a man of surprising genius. He was not a great thinker but he had many great thoughts. With an originality of mind which made him a pioneer in many fields, he combined a unique power of putting his thoughts into words which inspired his readers to action regardless of the conventions. He himself had no political experience, but the doctrine of The Social Contract as expounded by him provided the French Revolution with a potent ideology and fired its partisans to the creation of a new regime. Though he had taught little, and had been a failure in his teaching, the mixed treatise and story which described the education of the boy Emile and his wife-to-be Sophie, set all sorts of people educating Emiles and Sophies after his pattern, and gave education an entirely new direction. 'We have never seen in our own generation—indeed the world has not seen more than once or twice in all the course of history,' says Sir Henry Maine in his *Ancient Law*, 'a literature which has exercised such prodigious influence over the minds of men, over every cast and shade of intellect, as that which emanated from Rousseau between 1749 and 1762.'

Actually the education of Emile was not one that could be readily imitated except by people of rank whose children were brought up by tutors in private school rooms, and even they found imitation difficult, if not unsatisfactory. The wisest of his disciples were not long in discovering that the story was meant only by way of illustration, and that before they could apply the principles it illustrated they must work out methods appropriate to their own conditions. Kant, the greatest of the disciples, while agreeing with Rousseau regarding the badness of the schools of his own time and the need for a new education, was more concerned with public education than private, and advocated a natural education under expert teachers. Pestalozzi, through whom Rousseau's ideas passed into the life and work of the ordinary schools of Europe, based his new methods on the work of the good mother in the home, and analysed learning into its elements for the better instruction of children. From Pestalozzi the movement of reform was taken up by many practical educators like Froebel and Herbart, or by philosophers like Fichte, all of whom added creatively to the original tradition and gradually transformed it in different ways.

As the nineteenth century progressed, the *Emile* ceased to matter for most educators: partly because the kind of education it advocated was remote from the work of the schools which were being established for the masses of the people, partly because many of the ideas which had been revolutionary when first enunciated had been generally accepted and had come to be taken for granted as desirable even when not put into practice. The sentimentality, the exaggerations, the paradoxes, the contradictions which had served to arrest the attention of the first readers without detracting greatly from the truths they expressed, came in course of time to prejudice the issues for even sympathetic readers.

To the educators of the twentieth century, Rousseau is still to some extent foreign. But with the renaissance of the New Education and its spread over the world as a gospel for the healing of the nations, the writings of the first new educator have acquired a fresh value. This new education is still more a matter of principles than methods: it is in the very nature of the modern approach to teaching and discipline, that having set out to make education free and personal for the pupil, the teacher himself must in some measure work out the methods suitable for his special conditions. The guiding philosophy of the movement is consequently of greater consequence to all who are seeking to develop education along this course than any particular method. The perennial questions concerning community and individual, authority and freedom, adult and child, have all to be considered anew in reference to the work of home and school. Rousseau, it is obvious now, took a very one-sided view of these questions, but it was a one-sidedness that challenged and still challenges thought, since in the *Emile* he put the case for the child as the centre of educational concern as it had never been put before. Whatever more needs to be said by way of qualification, it is essential that the serious student of education should take account of those ideas of Rousseau which set Europe thinking in a new way about the preparation of children for the proper life of humanity.

What were these ideas? What truth of consequence is there in them? What is their practical value under present-day conditions? To these questions, I suggest, the reader should seek his or her own answer by a careful reading of the *Emile*, and possibly also of the other educational writings of Rousseau. In this book I have tried to make the task easier by abridgement and a new translation. The *Emile* is the kind of book which benefits, so far as the ordinary student is concerned, by considerable cutting. It is a somewhat discursive book, as Rousseau himself says in his Preface. He has an argument to unfold and a tale to tell in illustration of it, but he is always ready to go off on side lines, not specially relevant to his central theme. From the discussion of religious education in adolescence, he launches out on a long dissertation on natural religion which makes up about an eighth of the whole book: an excellent exposition but not really germane. The occasion of Emile's travels, again, leads to a summary of his *Social Contract*. And there are many such excursions of interest throughout the book quite worth reading for the understanding of Rousseau, but over all serving to hide the sequence of thought about education.

This sequence I have tried to make clear, not only by a selection of topics which includes most of what he has to say about education, but by the section headings which have been added to the text, and by the short introductions prefacing each of the five books. My own answers to the questions set forth above are given briefly at the end of the book, where the patient reader who has learned not to spoil a story by peeping at the last chapter will find them in due course, and be able to compare his conclusions with mine.

October 1955   **W. B.**

NOTE

In this edition Rousseau's text is set in larger type throughout, and the editor's commentary in smaller type.

THE AUTHOR'S PREFACE

THIS collection of reflections and comments, loosely strung together, was begun to please a good intelligent mother who was concerned about the education of her son. My first intention was to write a memoir of a few pages. But the subject ran away with me, and before I quite realised it the memoir had grown into a kind of book which was rather big for all that is in it but too small for its subject. After trying vainly to improve it I have decided that I ought to publish it as it stands in the hope of directing public attention to the matter. Even if my own ideas should prove bad, my labour will not have been in vain if I manage to stimulate good ones in other people.

I shall not say much about the importance of a good education or stop to demonstrate that the ordinary education is bad. A great many people have said that before me, and there is no need for me to fill a book with things that everybody knows. I will only remark that from time immemorial there has been constant complaint about the established practice but never a plan for anything better. In spite of all the writings that have the public utility for their aim, the first of all the utilities, which is the forming of man, continues to be overlooked.

Nothing is known about childhood. With our false ideas of it the more we do, the more we blunder. The wisest people are so much concerned with what grown ups should know that they never consider what children are capable of learning. They keep looking for the man in the child, not thinking of what he is before he becomes

5

a man. It is to this study I have given special thought, in the hope that even if my method should prove chimerical and false there will always be profit in my observations. I may have gone off wrong in my view of what is needed, but I believe I am right in my view of the person on whom we have to work. Begin then by studying your pupils better; for assuredly you do not know them. If you read the book with this in view I am sure you will find it quite useful.

It is with regard to what may be called the systematic part of the book, which simply follows the natural development of the child, that there is most chance of misunderstanding on the part of the reader. He will think he is reading the dreams of a visionary rather than a treatise on education. What can I do about it? It is not other people's ideas of education I am presenting but my own. It is a long standing reproach that I see things differently from other people. If sometimes I take a dogmatic tone it is not to force my views on the reader but just to talk to him as the thoughts come to me.

I am always being told to suggest something feasible. What in effect is being said to me is that I should propound the ordinary methods or at least combine something good with the existing evil. A plan like this is really more fantastic than mine, for in this combination the good gets spoiled and the bad is not cured. I would rather follow the established methods in their entirety and avoid the contradiction that would be produced in man by making for two discordant ends.

In every kind of project two things have to be considered. The first is the goodness of the project in itself; the second is the ease of execution. In the present case, the first question is whether the education I propose is suitable for mankind, and congenial to the human heart.

And is it practicable? That depends on the conditions under which it is tried. These conditions may vary indefinitely. The kind of education good for France will not suit Switzerland; that suitable for the middle classes will not suit the nobility. The greater or less ease of execution depends on a thousand circumstances which it is impossible to define except in a particular application of the method to this country or that, to this condition or that; and these particular applications are no part of my plan. All I am concerned with is that my plan should be capable of application wherever men are born. More I cannot promise.

INFANCY

Editorial Note

In the first drafts of the *Emile* circulated among Rousseau's friends nothing was said about the nursling stage. The book opened with the general discussion which now stands at the beginning of Book One and passed at once to the period of boyhood now dealt with in Book Two. One reader expostulated with him and suggested that he should tell about bringing up children from birth. His answer was that he knew nothing about the first stage of infant training. But under persuasion he proceeded to read about the subject and gather information from mothers of his acquaintance, and the outcome was an account of baby management which caught the imagination of his contemporaries and led many young mothers to reform their ways.

The First Book in its revised form deals with four main topics.

It begins with a general statement of Rousseau's ideas about education. These turn on the contrast between the goodness of man and the badness of man-made institutions: between the natural man, man in himself, and the man who lives in society, the citizen of some state. We must choose between making a man and making a citizen, he says, we cannot make both. With this as his premise Rousseau sets himself to show how by taking a child from birth and controlling his environment the original nature may be preserved unspoiled. He recognises that the child brought up in this way must one day become a member of society, and must indeed be prepared for it. To be a human being true to his own nature, he must be fitted to be in the world, but not of it. But there is no thought of this kind of training in the first instance: the time for it will come later. The first stage in a natural education takes place in the home, preferably under country conditions where the child will have the chance to grow up as simply as a peasant child, with no thought of anybody but himself.

Next, Rousseau introduces Emile, the fictitious pupil whose story gets interwoven with the abstract propositions of his treatise on education. There is not much to say about Emile at this point: the theme is the infant in general, not any particular infant. But by way of preparation for the subsequent stages, Rousseau has to explain how, contrary to his own conviction that the natural educators are the father and the mother (especially the father), he has assumed in the story the rôle of tutor, with the right to control all the conditions of the boy Emile's life.

Then follows a discussion of the care of children in the early months of life—the section added to the first versions of the book. It begins with an attempt to define the character of the infant mind. The child, in the early months, he says, has only vague feelings of pleasure and pain, but no senti-ments (definite feelings) and no ideas, till very gradually he makes contact with the external world through his sensations. The first education is largely a matter of giving him oppor-tunities for experiences of a varied kind. Most important for this is the method followed in dealing with his physical needs. The good mother is one who follows nature by suckling her own baby, and leaving him free from all restraints on his bodily movements. The essential thing is to make him a good healthy animal, by allowing him as much freedom as ever possible, after the example set by peasant mothers in the upbringing of their children. Whatever happens, he must never encounter resistance in grown-up wills, only in things.

Infancy comes to an end with the weaning of the child, the beginnings of speech, the first steps: all, about the same time. Once again the rule is to follow nature and be guided by peasant practice: not to hurry the weaning, to leave the child to make himself understood when he talks, to let him pick himself up when he falls, and pay no attention to his cries.

The Meaning of Education

Everything is good as it comes from the hands of the Maker of the world but degenerates once it gets into the hands of man. Man makes one land yield the products of another, disregards differences of climates, elements and seasons, mutilates his dogs and horses, perverts and disfigures everything. Not content to leave anything as nature has made it, he must needs shape man himself to his notions, as he does the trees in his garden.

But under present conditions, human beings would be even worse than they are without this fashioning. A man left entirely to himself from birth would be the most misshapen of creatures. Prejudices, authority, necessity, example, the social institutions in which we are immersed, would crush out nature in him without putting anything in its place. He would fare like a shrub that has grown up by chance in the middle of a road, and got trampled under foot by the passers-by.

Plants are fashioned by cultivation, men by education. We are born feeble and need strength; possessing nothing, we need assistance; beginning without intelligence, we need judgment. All that we lack at birth and need when grown up is given us by education. This education comes to us from nature, from men, or from things. The internal development of our faculties and organs is the education of nature. The use we learn to make of this development is the education of men. What comes to us from our experience of the things that affect us is the education of things. Each of us therefore is fashioned by three kinds of teachers. When their lessons are at variance the pupil is badly educated, and is never at peace with himself. When they coincide and lead to a common goal he goes straight to his mark and lives single-minded. Now, of these three educations the one due to nature is independent of us, and the one from things only depends on us to a limited extent. The education that comes from men is the only one within our control, and even that is doubtful. Who can hope to have the entire direction of the words and deeds of all the people around a child?

It is only by good luck that the goal can be reached. What is this goal? It is nature's own goal. Since the three educations must work together for a perfect result, the one that can be modified determines the course of the other two. But perhaps 'nature' is too vague a word. We must try to fix its meaning. Nature, it has been said, is only habit. Is that really so? Are there not habits which are formed under pressure, leaving the original nature unchanged? One example is the habit of plants which have been forced away from the upright direction. When set free, the plant retains the bent forced upon it; but the sap has not changed its first direction and any new growth the plant makes returns to the vertical. It is the same with human inclinations. So long as there is no change in conditions the inclinations due to habits, however unnatural, remain unchanged, but immediately the restraint is removed the habit vanishes and nature reasserts itself.

We are born capable of sensation and from birth are affected in diverse ways by the objects around us. As soon as we become conscious of our sensations we are inclined to seek or to avoid the objects which produce them: at first, because they are agreeable or disagreeable to us, later because we discover that they suit or do not suit us, and ultimately because of the judgments we pass on them by reference to the idea of happiness or perfection we get from reason. These inclinations extend and strengthen with the growth of sensibility and intelligence, but under the pressure of habit they are changed to some extent with our opinions. The inclinations before this change are what I call our nature. In my view everything ought to be in conformity with these original inclinations.

There would be no difficulty if our three educations were merely different. But what is to be done when they are at cross purposes? Consistency is plainly impossible when we seek to educate a man for others, instead of for himself. If we have to combat either nature or society, we must choose between making a man or making a citizen. We cannot make both. There is an inevitable conflict of aims, from which come two opposing forms of education: the one communal and public, the other individual and domestic.

To get a good idea of communal education, read Plato's *Republic*. It is not a political treatise, as those who merely judge books by their titles think. It is the finest treatise on education ever written. Communal education in this sense, however, does not and can not now exist. There are no longer any real fatherlands and therefore no real citizens. The words 'fatherland' and 'citizen' should be expunged from modern languages.

I do not regard the instruction given in those ridiculous establishments called colleges as 'public,' any more than the ordinary kind of education. This education makes for two opposite goals and reaches neither. The men it turns out are double-minded, seemingly concerned for others, but really only concerned for themselves. From this contradiction comes the conflict we never cease to experience in ourselves. We are drawn in different directions by nature and by man, and take a midway path that leads us nowhere. In this state of confusion we go through life and end up with our contradictions unsolved, never having been any good to ourselves or to other people.

There remains then domestic education, the education of nature. But how will a man who has been educated entirely for himself get on with other people? If there were any way of combining in a single person the twofold aim, and removing the contradictions of life, a great obstacle to happiness would be removed. But before passing judgment on this kind of man it would be necessary to follow his development and see him fully formed. It would be necessary, in a word, to make the acquaintance of the natural man. This is the subject of our quest in this book.

What can be done to produce this very exceptional person? In point of fact all we have to do is to prevent anything being done. When it is only a matter of sailing against the wind it is enough to tack, but when the sea runs high and you want to stay where you are, you must throw out the anchor.

In the social order where all stations in life are fixed, every one needs to be brought up for his own station. The individual who leaves the place for which he has been trained is useless in any other. In Egypt, where the son was obliged to follow in his father's footsteps, education had at least an assured aim: in our country where social ranks are fixed, but the men in them are constantly changing, nobody knows whether he is doing his son a good or a bad turn when he educates him for his own rank.

In the natural order where all men are equal, manhood is the common vocation. One who is well educated for that will not do badly in the duties that pertain to it. The fact that my pupil is intended for the army, the church or the bar, does not greatly concern me. Before the vocation determined by his parents comes the call of nature to the life of human kind. Life is the business I would have him learn. When he leaves my hands, I admit he will not be a magistrate, or a soldier, or a priest. First and foremost, he will be a man. All that a man must be he will be when the need arises, as well as anyone else. Whatever the changes of fortune he will always be able to find a place for himself.

The Natural Educators

It is not enough merely to keep children alive. They should be fitted to take care of themselves when they grow up. They should learn to bear the blows of fortune; to meet either wealth or poverty, to live if need be in the frosts of Iceland or on the sweltering rock of Malta. The important thing is not to ward off death, but to make sure they really live. Life is not just breathing: it is action, the functioning of organs, senses, faculties, every part of us that gives the consciousness of existence. The man who gets most out of life is not the one who has lived longest, but the one who has felt life most deeply.

Man's wisdom is but servile prejudice: his customs but subjection and restraint. From the beginning to the end of life civilised man is a slave. At birth he is sewn up in swaddling bands, and at death nailed down in a coffin. All through he is fettered by social institutions. 'Scarcely has the babe left his mother's womb and begun to enjoy the liberty of moving and stretching his limbs,' says Buffon, 'when new bonds are imposed on him. He is fastened in swaddling clothes, laid down with head fixed, legs outstretched, arms pinioned, and is prevented from moving by wrappings of cloth and bandages of all kinds.' The result is that the inner urge to bodily growth finds an insurmountable obstacle in the way of movements that are imperatively needed.

This irrational practice comes from a departure from nature. Mothers scorning their first duty are no longer willing to suckle their own children, and hand them over to hired nurses. These women, finding themselves mothers of strange children, lack the appeal of natural affection and are only concerned to save themselves bother. A child that has been left free needs constant watching; but if it is tightly bound it can be pitched into a corner where its cries will trouble no one. Do these fine mothers who get rid of their children and have a gay time in the city, realise the kind of treatment the swaddled babe is getting in the village?

The pretence is made that when children are left free they are likely to acquire wrong postures and to get misshapen limbs from their movements. This is one of the rationalisations of our false wisdom, and it is not borne out by experience. Children do not possess the strength that would make their movements dangerous to themselves, and the pain of a bad posture speedily warns them of the need for a change. We have not yet thought of swaddling puppies and kittens. Are they any the worse for this neglect? It is true that young children are clumsier, but they are also more feeble and can scarcely move. How could they injure themselves?

Let mothers deign to nurse their babies and a general reform of morals will follow as a matter of course. The natural sentiments will re-awaken in all hearts and the population will increase. With the home a place of happy life the domestic tasks become the dearest occupations of the wife and the finest diversions of the husband. Once women become good mothers, men will not be long in becoming good husbands and fathers.

No mother, no child. Their duties are reciprocal: failure on the one side leads to a neglect of duty on the other. The child's love for his mother should precede any sense of obligation. If the call of the blood is not strengthened by habit and nurture, it fades out in the early years and the heart (one might say) dies still-born. We have taken the first steps away from nature.

There is a departure from nature in the opposite direction when a woman makes an idol of her child, and carries care to excess by trying to save him from the hard knocks that come in the way of nature. Thetis, says the story, plunged her son into the waters of Styx to make him invulnerable. This is an allegory with an obvious moral. The unkind mothers of whom I am speaking take the other course. By plunging their children into softness they lay up trouble for them.

Observe nature and follow the path she marks out. She keeps on disciplining the children all the time. She hardens their temperaments by ordeals of every kind. She shows them the meaning of pain and suffering in their early years. Their teeth as they come through give them fever. Sharp colics cause convulsions. Racking coughs choke them. Worms torment them. Ferments in the blood cause dangerous eruptions. Early childhood is beset with sickness and danger. Half the children born die before eight. It is only after the child has succeeded in passing these tests and has won through to strength that life becomes more secure.

This is nature's way. Why set yourself against it? Do you not see that in attempting to improve on her work you are destroying it and defeating the provision she has made? So long as you do not go beyond the measure of the child's strength there is less risk in employing it than in husbanding it. Train the children, then, for the hardships they will one day have to endure. Harden them to the rigours of the seasons, the climate, the elements. Inure them to hunger, thirst and fatigue. Dip them in the waters of Styx.

The babe comes into the world with a cry, and his first days are spent in tears. Sometimes he is dandled and caressed to soothe him. At other times he is threatened and beaten to keep him quiet. Either we do what pleases him, or we make him do what pleases us. He gives orders, or he gets them: there is no middle way for us. His first ideas are either of mastery or of servitude. Before he can speak he commands: before he can act he obeys. Sometimes he is punished for faults before he knows anything about them and even before he is able to commit them. That is how we put into the young heart the passions we afterwards impute to nature. Having taken pains to make the child bad we complain about his badness.

If you want the child to keep his original character watch over him from the moment he enters the world. Get hold of him as soon as he is born and never leave him till he is a man. Short of that, you will not succeed. Just as the right nurse is the mother, the right teacher is the father. A child will be better brought up by a wise father however limited, than by the cleverest teacher in the world. Zeal makes up for lack of talent—better than talent does for lack of zeal.

A father has only done a third of his duty when he begets children and makes provision for them. To his species he owes men; to society he owes social beings; to the state he owes citizens. Every person who fails to pay this triple debt is blameworthy, even more so if he only pays it in part. The man who cannot fulfil a father's duties has no right to become a father. Neither poverty nor business nor concern for public opinion exempts him from the obligation to look after his children and educate them himself.

But what does this rich man, this busy head of a family, who is compelled, as he says, to neglect his children do? He pays another man to do his work. You mercenary creature! Do you think you can buy your son a father-substitute with your money? Make no mistake. It is not a teacher but a lackey you are giving him; and this fellow will not be long in making another lackey.

There has been much discussion about the qualities of a good tutor. The first essential is that he should not be a hired man. There are some callings so noble that the man who undertakes them for money shows himself unworthy of them. Teaching is one of them. 'Who then will bring up my child?' I have told you: yourself. 'I cannot.' You cannot. Then get a friend to act for you. I see no other solution.

The more I think of it, the more fresh difficulties present themselves. The tutor would have to be specially educated for the education he is to conduct, and the servants would have to be educated for their young master, so that all those who come near the child would themselves acquire the impressions they are to impart to him. It would be necessary, in fact, to pass back from education to education ever so far. How can a child be well educated unless by one who is well educated himself? Can this rare mortal be found? I do not know. I suspect that the father who realises fully the value of a good tutor will prefer to do without one and undertake the task himself.

Emile and his Tutor

A man of high rank once suggested that I should be his son's tutor. But having had experience already I knew myself unfit and I refused. Instead of the difficult task of educating a child, I now undertake the easier task of writing about it. To provide details and examples in illustration of my views and to avoid wandering off into airy speculations, I propose to set forth the education of Emile, an imaginary pupil, from birth to manhood. I take for granted that I am the right man for the duties in respect of age, health, knowledge and talents.

A tutor is not bound to his charge by the ties of nature as the father is, and so is entitled to choose his pupil, especially when as in this case he is providing a model for the education of other children. I assume that Emile is no genius, but a boy of ordinary ability: that he is the inhabitant of some temperate climate, since it is only in temperate climates that human beings develop completely; that he is rich, since it is only the rich who have need of the natural education that would fit them to live under all conditions; that he is to all intents and purposes an orphan, whose tutor having undertaken the parents' duties will also have their right to control all the circumstances of his upbringing; and, finally, that he is a vigorous, healthy, well-built child.

The new born child needs a nurse. The best nurse would be the mother if she were prepared to take her instructions from the tutor. In any case only one person should have charge of the child throughout the period of education. There should be no change in the persons responsible, and no conflict of authority. If the nurse is to be a stranger great care should be taken with the choice. In order to secure good milk she must have had a child of her own quite recently, and be healthy in temperament as well as in body. Instead of bringing a country woman into the crowded town the boy should be sent to the country to live amid fresh air in his foster mother's cottage, away from the disease and vice of the man-devouring town.

It is the custom to bathe infants in warm water. That is a concession in the first instance to the effeminacy of the parents. As the child grows stronger the heat of the water should be gradually decreased, till finally the child is bathed in ice cold water, both summer and winter. From the beginning tight clothes should be avoided. Dress him in loose flannel wrappings which allow free movement and let the air play about his body. Put him in a well padded room with plenty of opportunity to move about, and when he grows stronger leave him to crawl about the floor. You will see him growing sturdier every day.

The Beginnings of Education

We are born with a capacity for learning, but know nothing and distinguish nothing. The mind is cramped by imperfect half-formed organs and has not even the consciousness of its own existence. The movements and cries of the new born child are purely mechanical, quite devoid of understanding and will.

Children's first sensations are wholly in the realm of feeling. They are only aware of pleasure and pain. With walking and grasp undeveloped, it takes a long time for them to construct the representative sensations which acquaint them with external objects; but even before these objects reach up to and depart from their eyes, if one may put it so, the recurrence of the sensations begins to subject them to the bondage of habit. You see their eyes always turning to the light and unconsciously taking the direction from which the light comes, so that you have to be careful to keep them facing the light in order to prevent them acquiring a squint or becoming cross-eyed. Similarly, they have to be accustomed quite early to darkness, or soon they will wail and cry if they find themselves in the dark. Food and sleep, if too precisely organised, come to be necessary at definite intervals, and soon the desire for them is due not to need but to habit. Or rather, habit adds a new need to that of nature. That is something to be avoided.

The only habit the child should be allowed to acquire is to contract none. He should not be carried on one arm more than the other or allowed to make use of one hand more than the other, or to want to eat, sleep or do things at definite hours; and he should be able to remain alone by night or day. Prepare in good time for the reign of freedom and the exercise of his powers, by allowing his body its natural habits and accustoming him always to be his own master and follow the dictates of his will as soon as he has a will of his own.

When the child begins to distinguish objects, careful choice must be made of those to be brought to his notice. Everything new is naturally interesting. Man feels himself so feeble that he dreads anything unfamiliar. The habit of seeing new things without emotion destroys this dread. Children brought up in well kept houses where spiders are not tolerated are afraid of spiders, and the fear often lasts when they grow up. I have never seen a peasant, man, woman or child, afraid of spiders.

Since the mere choice of the objects put before a child can make him timid or brave, why not begin his education before he can talk and understand? I would like him to be habituated to the sight of new things and strange ugly creatures, but gradually and at a distance until he is accustomed to them. No objects are frightsome to those who see them every day.

When at the parting of Andromache and Hector the little Astyanax is scared by the waving plumes on his father's helmet and does not recognise him, and throws himself weeping into his nurse's arms, what is to be done to deliver him from this terror? Just what Hector does: put the helmet on the ground and caress the child. In a calmer moment one would not stop there. One would go up to the helmet, play with the plumes, get the child to handle them. Then the nurse would pick up the helmet and put it laughingly on her own head, if perchance a woman dared touch Hector's armour.

I have noticed that children are rarely afraid of thunder unless the claps are terrible and actually hurt the ear. Otherwise this fear only affects them when they know that the thunder sometimes hurts or kills. When reason brings fear, reassurance comes through habit. By slow careful gradations man and child alike can be made absolutely intrepid.

At the beginning of life when memory and imagination are still inactive the child attends only to what actually affects his senses. Since his sensations are the primary material of knowledge, the presentation of them in proper order prepares the memory for delivering them in the same order to the understanding later on. But as the child only attends to his sensations, it is sufficient in the first instance to show him very distinctly the connection of these sensations with the objects which cause them. He wants to touch and handle everything. Put no obstacle in the way of his restless movements. He learns to feel heat, cold, hardness, softness, weight, and comes to judge of the size and shape of bodies and all their sensory qualities, by looking at them, fingering them, listening to them, above all by comparing sight and touch.

It is only when we move that we learn that there are

things other than ourselves, and come to the idea of space. It is because the child lacks this idea that he reaches out his hand indifferently to grasp the object that touches him or the object a hundred paces off. This effort of his looks like him ordering the object to come to him, or ordering you to bring it. Nothing of the kind. It is simply that the object he sees at first in his brain and then on his eyes now appears at the end of his arms: he has no picture of any space beyond his reach. At this stage when you take him walks, be careful to lift him from place to place and make him aware of the change of position so that he may learn to judge distances. As soon as he knows distances the method needs to be changed. He must then be carried not as pleases him, but as pleases you. For once he is no longer misled by his senses, there is a remarkable change in the motive of his effort.

Man's first state being one of misery and weakness, the first utterances are wailing and weeping. Feeling his needs and being unable to satisfy them, the child implores the help of others by his cries. When he is hungry or thirsty he weeps. When too hot or too cold, he weeps. When he needs to move and is kept quiet, he weeps. When he wants to sleep and is kept awake, he weeps. He has only one language because he has only one kind of discomfort. His imperfect organs make no distinction among different impressions. All his troubles produce the one sensation of suffering.

From these weepings which seem so little worthy of our attention comes the first relation of man to his environment. Here is forged the first link in the long chain that constitutes the social order. When the child cries there is something wrong with him, something he needs and cannot get. You examine him, you try to discover the need, you find it, you put things right. When you do not find it or cannot put things right, the weeping goes on, importunately. The child is petted to make him quiet, he is rocked or sung to sleep. If he is obstinate you get impatient and threaten him. Brutal nurses sometimes strike him. Strange lessons these as an introduction to life!

The disposition of children to resentment and rage calls for very special care. Make sure that servants who provoke and irritate them are kept at a distance. They are a hundred times more deadly than exposure to air and weather. So long as children find resistance only in things and not in human wills, they will not become obstinate and bad tempered, and will enjoy good health. At the same time it is necessary to keep in mind the difference between obeying the children and not thwarting them. Their first tears are prayers: if we are not on our guard they soon become orders. They begin by getting assistance, they end by getting service. Thus through the very weakness from which comes the sense of dependence there springs later the idea of mastery and domination, excited less by their needs than by our services. Here begin to appear moral effects, the immediate cause of which is not in nature. It is already evident at this early age how important it is to interpret rightly the intention behind the gesture or the cry.

The Weaning of the Child

Children are weaned too soon. The time for weaning is indicated by the cutting of the teeth. At this stage the child instinctively puts everything he gets into his mouth and chews it. To make the operation easy some people give him a hard article like ivory or a wolf's tooth for a plaything. That in my judgment is a mistake. Young puppies do not exercise their baby teeth on pebbles, iron or bone, but on wood, leather and rags, all soft yielding materials on which the teeth can leave their mark. The important thing is to get the child accustomed to chewing his food from the beginning. That is the right way to help with the cutting of the teeth; and then when he begins to swallow, the salivary juices mixed with the food help digestion. I would have children begin by chewing dried fruit and crusts and give them little sticks of dry bread or biscuits. After they have managed to soften this in the mouth they will swallow a little of it. The teeth will come through and they will find themselves weaned almost before they know it. Peasants have good digestions and that is how they are weaned.

The Beginnings of Speech

Children hear things said to them from birth. We talk to them not only before they understand what is said to them, but before they can reproduce the words they hear. I have no objection to the nurse amusing the child with a variety of lively songs and sounds, but I object to her stupefying him with a host of meaningless words. The first articulate words he hears should be few, simple, clear and often repeated, and should refer only to objects that can be shown to him. The unfortunate fluency in the use of words that are not understood begins sooner than we realise. The scholar listens to the verbiage of his teacher in school just as he listened to the babblings of the nurse in his cradle. In my opinion, it would be better for his education if he were brought up with nothing of this.

A whole crowd of reflections present themselves when one begins to consider the structure of language and the first utterances of children. To begin with, they have their own kind of grammar, with a syntax which has rules more general than ours. If you pay careful attention you will be surprised at the precision with which they follow certain analogies, that are only inadmissable because they are contrary to usage. It is an intolerable piece of pedantry to correct all these little faults. There is no fear of the children not correcting them for themselves in good time. Always speak correctly in their presence and you can be sure that without any criticism on your part their language will be unconsciously refined on the model of yours.

A quite different evil, just as easy to prevent, is the pressure put on them to begin to talk. This indiscreet insistence produces the opposite effect from what is intended. It leads them to speak later and less distinctly. The close attention paid to all they say makes it unnecessary for them to articulate properly. They scarcely deign to open their mouths and many of them retain a minced, mumbling, almost unintelligible speech all their lives.

I have lived a great deal among peasants, and I have never heard one of them speak thickly. Why is this? Are their organs differently fashioned from ours? Oh no, but they get a different training. In front of my window is a hillock on which the children of the place gather for their games. Though they are at a considerable distance from me I hear distinctly all they say. Every day my ear misleads me concerning their age. I hear the voices of ten-year-old children, but what I see is the stature and looks of children of three or four. This is due to the fact that up to the age of five or six, town children brought up in a room under the eye of a governess do not need to speak out to make themselves heard. It is quite different in the country. A peasant woman is not always beside her children. If they want to make themselves heard they must speak loudly and distinctly. That is the right way to learn pronunciation.

I agree that the common people and the villagers make their own mistakes. Almost always they speak too loudly and coarsely; their accent is too marked, their words are badly chosen, and so forth. But these petty faults of speech which we are so afraid of our children picking up are really of no consequence. They can be prevented or corrected with the greatest ease. What can never be corrected are the faults of low, confused and faltering speech which we produce in them by constant criticism of their tone and language.

The child who is learning to speak should hear only words he can understand, and use only words he can pronounce. When he begins to lisp do not trouble to guess what he is saying. To expect to be always listened to is a form of domination which a child has no right to enjoy. It should be enough to make adequate provision for his needs: it is for him to make you understand anything beyond that. There is even less point in being in a hurry to get him to talk. He will learn to speak well enough himself, as soon as he comes to appreciate the use of it.

The real evil in premature speech is that children's words have a different meaning from ours, and the result is mutual misunderstanding. Their vocabulary should be kept as restricted as possible. It is a great disadvantage for them to have more words than ideas and be able to say more than they think.

Learning to Walk

Our pedantic eagerness to instruct is always leading us to teach children what they can learn better for themselves, and to forget the things they need to be taught. Is there anything more foolish than the pains we take to teach them to walk when there has never yet been a child who failed to walk by reason of his nurse's neglect? Think rather of the many people who walk badly all their lives, because they have been taught to walk badly. Emile will have no pads or go-carts or leading strings. Instead of being cooped up in a stuffy room he will be taken out to the fields every day. There he will run and gambol and tumble a hundred times a day. The oftener he falls the better. He will soon learn to pick himself up. The blessedness of freedom makes up for many bruises.

The first developments of childhood all come about the same time. The child learns to eat, to speak and to walk almost simultaneously. This brings to an end the first epoch of his life. Before this time he is little different from what he was in his mother's body. He has neither feelings nor ideas, and scarcely even sensations. He has not even the sense of his own existence. *Vivit et est vitae nescius ipse suae.* (Ovid, *Trist.* 1.)

BOOK TWO

BOYHOOD

Editorial Note

In the Second Book, Rousseau gets down to the problem of education as it concerns the boy up to the age of twelve. Natural education is education that takes proper account of the pupil's nature in its different aspects. Boys are different from girls and must be educated differently. (This is discussed in Book Five.) Every child is different from every other and must be educated differently. (This is discussed in the *New Heloise*, V 3.) In the *Emile*, the difference mainly stressed is the difference between age periods, each of which according to Rousseau has its own distinctive character and comes to its own maturity. It is his conscious endeavour in the Five Books of the *Emile* to define as well as he can the corresponding stages of growth in sociological and psychological terms. The baby of Book One is at the animal stage. The boy of Book Two is comparable with the savage: the boy Emile has to learn, as the noble savage of Rousseau's imagination learns, through direct experience in varied practical activities connected with his interests and needs. Psychological characterisation of the successive ages is based on the idea of emerging faculties. According to Rousseau the boy lacks the ability to compare and relate facts, and so has no true ideas. His thinking all goes on in the sphere of the senses. The senses give him images of the facts with which he has to deal, and he can check up the information given by one sense with that given by the other senses. This concrete kind of thinking suffices for all the purposes of his limited life. Actually there is a certain anticipation of the adult understanding and the ideas with which it works in the sentiments (or definite feelings) relating to the facts of experience. In the sphere of

30

conduct self-love (*amour de soi*) concerned only with his own interests is the dominant motive. Self-esteem (*amour propre*) which comes into play in one's relations with other people is, or should be, of little consequence at this pre-social stage.

The fact that the reason is not yet operative has important educational consequences. Lacking proper understanding the child under twelve is very much at the mercy of his social environment. His opinions about things are the opinions of family and associates. His conduct depends on what they tell him he ought to do. The only way to keep him true to his own nature is to withdraw him from the artificial life of society and bring him up under conditions controlled in the interests of his education by a tutor who devotes his whole life to the task. And the education he gets under these conditions must be negative rather than positive. It is much more important to exclude vice and error than to inculcate virtue and truth. Until such time as he becomes a rational being and can make virtue and truth his own by personal acquirement he must be kept in the world of the senses. He must learn to do right, not as something that ought to be done to adult order, but as something he must do if he is to escape the painful consequences of wrong action. In the same way he must be limited to such ideas as are obvious to him through his senses. In geometry, for example, he can see the equality of a figure which can be superimposed on another, but can give no rational justification: geometry is an art of seeing at this stage, not an art of reasoning. Geography, history, languages and literature are all beyond his undeveloped understanding, and can only be taught as verbal knowledge. The less the boy learns about such studies and all that pertains to the facts of social life the better.

The End of Infancy

At this point begins the second phase of life. Infancy in the literal sense of the word is over. The child is no longer an 'infant', but a boy.

When children commence to speak they weep less. One language takes the place of another. Once they can say in words that they suffer there is no reason for saying it with cries, unless the suffering is beyond expression in words. If they go on weeping after this, it is the people around them that are to blame. It will need to be a very severe pain that makes Emile weep after he has said 'I am hurt'. So long as he cries I do not go to him. I run to him as soon as he is quiet. Before long his way of summoning me will be to be quiet or at most to utter a single cry. If he falls or bumps his head or gets a bloody nose I will not fuss about him and show alarm. For a time at least I will keep perfectly calm. The mischief is done. He must just endure it. Fuss on my part will only frighten him more and add to his troubles. It is at this age that the child gets his first lessons in courage and comes to learn to endure great sufferings by meeting light ones fearlessly.

So far from trying to protect Emile from hurts I should be sorry if he never got hurt and grew up without knowledge of pain. Suffering should be his first lesson. It is the one he will most need to learn. It looks as if children were young and feeble to give them the chance of learning these important lessons without danger. The child who falls his own height will not break a leg. If he strikes himself with a stick he will not break his arm. When he grasps a sharp knife he will not press it hard enough to cut himself badly. I have never heard of a child left alone killing himself or doing himself serious harm, unless he had been left foolishly on a high place, or near a fire, or within reach of dangerous instruments.

Happiness in Childhood

Another advance at this time which makes crying less necessary is increase in strength. The more children can do for themselves the less help they need from other people. Added strength brings with it the sense needed for its direction. With the coming of self-consciousness at this second stage individual life really begins. Memory extends the sense of identity over all the moments of the child's existence. He becomes one and the same person, capable of happiness or sorrow. From this point on it is essential to regard him as a moral being.

Though we know fairly well the extreme length of human life and the chance of reaching it at any particular age, nothing is more uncertain than the prospects of life for any one person. Very few reach the full term. The greatest risks are at the beginning. Of all the children born a bare half survive at adolescence, and it is improbable that your pupil will reach manhood. In view of this, what are we to think of the barbarous education which sacrifices the present to an uncertain future and makes the child miserable in order to prepare him for a remote happiness which he will probably not live to enjoy?

Your first duty is to be humane. Love childhood. Look with friendly eyes on its games, its pleasures, its amiable dispositions. Which of you does not sometimes look back regretfully on the age when laughter was ever on the lips and the heart free of care? Why steal from the little innocents the enjoyment of a time that passes all too quickly?

Already I hear the clamour of the false wisdom that regards the present as of no account and is for ever chasing a future which flees as we advance. This is the time to correct the evil inclinations of mankind, you reply. Suffering should be increased in childhood when it is least felt, to reduce it at the age of reason. But how do you know that all the fine lessons with which you oppress the feeble mind of the child will not do more harm than good? Can you prove that these bad tendencies you profess to be correcting are not due to your own misguided efforts rather than to nature?

If we are to keep in touch with reality we must never forget what befits our condition. Humanity has its place in the scheme of things. Childhood has its place in the scheme of human life. We must view the man as a man, and the child as a child. The best way to ensure human well-being is to give each person his place in life and keep him there, regulating the passions in accordance with the individual constitution. The rest depends on external factors outwith our control.

We can never know absolute good or evil. Everything in this life is mixed. We never experience a pure sentiment, or remain in the same state for two successive moments. Weal and woe are common to us all, but in differing measure. The happiest man is the one who suffers least: the most miserable the one who has least pleasure. Always the sufferings outweigh the enjoyments. The felicity of man here below is therefore a negative state, to be measured by the fewness of his ills. Every feeling of pain is inseparable from the desire to escape from it: every idea of pleasure inseparable from the desire for its enjoyment. Privation is implicit in desire, and all privations are painful. Consequently unhappiness consists in the excess of desire over power. A conscious being whose powers equalled his desires would be absolutely happy.

In what then does the human wisdom that leads to true happiness consist? Not simply in the diminution of desires, for if they fell below our power to achieve, part of our faculties would be unemployed and our entire being would not be satisfied. Neither does it consist in the extension of our faculties, for a disproportionate increase in our desires would only make us more miserable. True happiness comes with equality of power and will. The only man who gets his own way is the one who does not need another's help to get it: from which it follows that the supreme good is not authority, but freedom. The true freeman wants only what he can get, and does only what pleases him. This is my fundamental maxim. Apply it to childhood and all the rules of education follow.

There are two kinds of dependence: dependence on things, which is natural, and dependence on men, which is social. Dependence on things being non-moral is not prejudicial to freedom and engenders no vices: dependence on men being capricious engenders them all. The only cure for this evil in society would be to put the law in place of the individual, and to arm the general will with a real power that made it superior to every individual will.

Keep the child in sole dependence on things and you will follow the natural order in the course of his education. Put only physical obstacles in the way of indiscreet wishes and let his punishments spring from his own actions. Without forbidding wrong-doing, be content to prevent it. Experience or impotence apart from anything else should take the place of law for him. Satisfy his desires, not because of his demands but because of his needs. He should have no consciousness of obedience when he acts, nor of mastery when someone acts for him. Let him experience liberty equally in his actions and in yours.

Be specially careful not to give the child empty formulae of politeness, to serve as magic words for subjecting his surroundings to his will and getting him what he wants at once. For my part I am less afraid of rudeness than of arrogance in Emile, and would rather have him say 'Do this' as a request, than 'Please' as a command. I am not concerned with the words he uses, but with what they imply.

Excessive severity and excessive indulgence are equally to be avoided. If you let children suffer you endanger health and life. If you are over-careful in shielding them from trouble of every kind you are laying up much unhappiness for the future: you are withdrawing them from the common lot of man, to which they must one day become subject in spite of you.

You will tell me that I am making the same mistake as those bad fathers whom I blamed for sacrificing their children's happiness for the sake of a distant time that may never come. That is not so, for the liberty I allow my pupil amply compensates for the slight hardships I let him experience. I see little scamps playing in the snow, blue and stiff with cold and scarcely able to move a finger. There is nothing to hinder them warming themselves, but they don't. If they were forced to come indoors they would feel the rigours of constraint a hundred times more than the cold. What then is there to complain about? Am I making the child unhappy by exposing him to hardships which he is quite willing to endure? I am doing him good at the present moment by leaving him free. I am doing him good in the future by arming him against inevitable evils. If he had to choose between being my pupil or yours, do you think he would hesitate for an instant?

The surest way to make your child unhappy is to accustom him to get everything he wants. With desire constantly increasing through easy satisfaction, lack of power will sooner or later force you to a refusal in spite of yourself, and the unwonted refusal will cause him deeper annoyance than the mere lack of what he desires. First he will want the stick in your hand, then the bird that flies past, then the star that shines above him. Everything he sees he will want: and unless you were God you could never hope to satisfy him. How could such a child possibly be happy? Happy! He is a despot, at once the meanest of slaves and the most wretched of creatures. Let us get back to the primitive way. Nature made children to be loved and helped, not to be obeyed and feared. Is there in the world a being more feeble and unhappy, more at the mercy of his environment, more in need of pity and protection than a child? Surely then there is nothing more offensive or more unseemly than the sight of a dictatorial headstrong child, issuing orders to those around him and assuming the tone of a master to people without whom he would perish.

On the other hand, it should be obvious that with the many restrictions imposed on children by their own weakness it is barbarous for us to add subjection to our caprices to the natural subjection, and take from them such limited liberty as they possess. Social servitude will come with the age of reason. Why anticipate it by a domestic servitude? Let one moment of life be free from this yoke which nature has not imposed, and leave the child to the enjoyment of his natural liberty.

The Law of Necessity

I come back to practice. I have already said that what your child gets he should get because he needs it, not because he asks for it, and that he should never act from obedience but only from necessity. For this reason, the words 'obey' and 'command' must be banished from his vocabulary, still more the words 'duty' and 'obligation'; but 'force', 'necessity', 'weakness' and 'constraint' should be emphasised. It is impossible to form any idea of moral facts or social relations before the age of reason. Consequently the use of terms which express such ideas should as far as possible be avoided, for fear the child comes to attach to these words false ideas which cannot or will not be eradicated at a later time.

'Reason with children' was Locke's chief maxim. It is the one most popular today, but it does not seem to me justified by success. For my part I do not see any children more stupid than those who have been much reasoned with. Of all the human faculties, reason which may be said to be compounded of all the rest develops most slowly and with greatest difficulty. Yet it is reason that people want to use in the development of the first faculties. A reasonable man is the masterwork of a good education: and we actually pretend to be educating children by means of reason! That is beginning at the end. If children appreciated reason they would not need to be educated.

Instead of appealing to reason, say to the child: 'You must not do that!' 'Why not?' 'Because it is wrong.' 'Why is it wrong?' 'Because it is forbidden.' 'Why is it forbidden?' 'Because it is wrong.' That is the inevitable circle. To distinguish right from wrong and appreciate the reason for the duties of man is beyond a child's powers.

Nature wants children to be children before they are men. If we deliberately depart from this order we shall get premature fruits which are neither ripe nor well flavoured and which soon decay. We shall have youthful sages and grown up children. Childhood has ways of seeing, thinking and feeling peculiar to itself: nothing can be more foolish than to seek to substitute our ways for them. I should as soon expect a child of ten to be five feet in height as to be possessed of judgment.

Treat your pupil according to his age. Begin by putting him in his place and keep him in it so firmly that he will not think of leaving it. Then he will practice the most important lesson of wisdom before he knows what wisdom is. Give him absolutely no orders of any kind. Do not even let him imagine that you claim any authority over him. Let him only know that he is weak and you are strong, and that therefore he is at your mercy. Quite early let him feel the heavy yoke which nature imposes on man, the yoke of the necessity in things as opposed to human caprice. If there is anything he should not do, do not forbid him, but prevent him without explanation or reasoning. Whatever you give, give at the first word without prayers or entreaty, and above all without conditions. Give with pleasure, refuse with regret, but let your refusals be irrevocable. Your 'No' once uttered must be a wall of brass which the child will stop trying to batter down once he has exhausted his strength on it five or six times.

It is strange that all the time people have been bringing up children nobody has thought of any instruments for their direction but emulation, jealousy, envy, vanity, greed or base fear; most dangerous passions all of them, sure to corrupt the soul. Foolish teachers think they are working wonders when they are simply making the children wicked in the attempt to teach them about goodness. Then they announce gravely: such is man. Yes, such is the man you have made. All the instruments have been tried but one, and that as it happens is the only one that can succeed: well regulated liberty.

Avoid verbal lessons with your pupil. The only kind of lesson he should get is that of experience. Never inflict any punishment, for he does not know what it is to be at fault. Being devoid of all morality in his actions he can do nothing morally wrong, nothing that deserves either punishment or reprimand.

Let us lay it down as an incontestable principle that the first impulses of nature are always right. There is no original perversity in the human heart. Of every vice we can say how it entered and whence it came. The only passion natural to man is self-love, or self-esteem in a broad sense. This self-esteem has no necessary reference to other people. In so far as it relates to ourselves it is good and useful. It only becomes good or bad in the social application we make of it. Until reason, which is the guide of self-esteem, makes its appearance, the child should not do anything because he is seen or heard by other people, but only do what nature demands of him. Then he will do nothing but what is right.

I do not mean to say that he will never do any mischief: that he will never hurt himself, for example, or break a valuable bit of furniture. He might do a great deal that was bad without being bad, because the wrong action depends on harmful intention and that he will never have. When children are left free to blunder it is better to remove everything that would make blundering costly, and not leave anything fragile and precious within reach. Their room should be furnished with plain solid furniture, without mirrors, china or ornaments. My Emile whom I am bringing up in the country will have nothing in his room to distinguish it from that of a peasant. If in spite of your precautions the child manages to upset things and break some useful articles, do not punish or scold him for your own negligence. Do not even let him guess that he has annoyed you. Behave as if the furniture had got broken of itself. Consider you have done very well if you can avoid saying anything.

Negative Education: (1) *No Moral Instruction*

May I set forth at this point the most important and the most useful rule in all education? It is not to save time but to waste it. The most dangerous period in human life is that between birth and the age of twelve. This is the age when errors and vices sprout, before there is any instrument for their destruction. When the instrument is available the roots have gone too deep to be extracted. The mind should remain inactive till it has all its faculties.

It follows from this that the first education should be purely negative. It consists not in teaching virtue and truth, but in preserving the heart from vice and the mind from error. If you could do nothing and let nothing be done, so that your pupil came to the age of twelve strong and healthy but unable to distinguish his right hand from his left, the eyes of his understanding would be open to reason from your very first lessons. In the absence of both prejudices and habits there would be nothing in him to oppose the effects of your teaching and care.

Do the opposite of what is usually done and you will almost always be right. Fathers and teachers, anxious to make a learned doctor instead of a child, correct, reprove, flatter, threaten, instruct, reason. There is a better way. Be reasonable and do not reason with your pupil. It is a mistake to try to get him to approve of things he dislikes. To bring reason into what is disagreeable at this stage will only discredit it. Exercise body, senses, powers, but keep the mind inactive as long as possible. Let childhood ripen in children.

The practical value of this method is confirmed by consideration of the distinctive genius of the child. Each mind has a form of its own in conformity with which it must be directed. If you are a wise man you will observe your pupil carefully before saying a word to him. In the first instance leave his essential character full liberty to manifest itself, in order to get a better view of his whole personality.

But where are we to place this child of ours when we are bringing him up like an automaton unaffected by anything outside himself? Must we keep him up in the moon or in some desert island? Are we to separate him from all human beings? Will he not see other children of his own age? Will he not see his relatives, his neighbours, his nurse, his lackey, even his tutor, who will assuredly be no angel? This is a very substantial objection. I have never pretended that it was easy to make education natural. Perhaps the difficulties are insurmountable. I do not say that anyone will reach the goal I have set, but I do say that the one who comes nearest will succeed best.

Remember that before you dare undertake the making of a man you must be a man yourself. While the child is as yet without knowledge of the world there is still time to make sure that everything around him is proper for him to see. To ensure this you must make yourself worthy of the respect and love of everybody, so that all will seek to please you. You will not be the child's master unless you are master of everything that surrounds him. This is another reason for bringing Emile up in the country, far from the filthy morals of the towns. The glitter of town life is seductive and corrupting while the gross vices of country people are more likely to repel than to seduce. In a village the tutor will be in much better control of the objects he wants the child to see. If he is helpful to the people, they will all be eager to oblige him and appear to his pupil as if they were in reality what the master would like them to be. If they do not correct their vices, they will at any rate refrain from scandalous behaviour, and that is all that is wanted for our purpose.

Be simple and hold yourself in check, you zealous teachers. Never be in a hurry to act. So far as you can, refrain from a good instruction for fear of giving a bad one. Since you cannot prevent the child learning from the examples set by others, confine your care to impressing these examples on his mind in the form which suits him best. The impetuous passions have a great effect on the child who witnesses them. Anger is so noisy in its expression that it cannot but be noticed by any one near. Here is obviously a chance for a pedagogue to concoct a fine discourse. But no fine discourses for you: not a word. Leave the child to come to you. Astounded by the sight of an angry man he will be sure to ask questions. Your answer is simple. It is suggested by the very things that have struck the senses. He sees an inflamed countenance, flashing eyes, threatening gestures; he hears cries: all signs that something is wrong with the body. Tell him quietly: 'The poor man is ill, he has an attack of fever.' Such an idea if given at the proper time will have as salutary effects as the most long-winded discourse, and it will have useful applications later on. On this way of thinking you are entitled, if the necessity arises, to treat a rebellious child as an invalid. You can confine him to his room, perhaps send him to bed, put him on a diet, and so make him afraid of his budding vices without him ever regarding the severity you are perhaps forced to use for their cure as a punishment. And should it happen that in a moment of heat you lose your own composure and moderation do not try to hide your faults. Just say to him frankly with a tender reproach: 'You have made me ill.'

My plan is not to go into details, but only to set forth general principles and gives examples in difficult cases. I do not think it is possible to bring up a child to the age of twelve in society without giving him some idea of the relations of man to man and the moral aspects of human conduct. The best one can do is to postpone these necessary notions as long as possible, and when they can be no longer postponed to limit them to the immediate requirement.

Our first duties are to ourselves. Self is the centre of the primitive sentiments. The natural impulses all relate in the first instance to our preservation and well-being. Hence the first sentiment of justice does not come to us from what we owe others, but from what others owe us. It is another of the blunders of the ordinary education to talk to children about their duties, and say nothing about their rights. This takes them beyond their comprehension and their interest.

The first idea a child should have given him is not that of liberty but of property. To get that he must possess something of his own. To tell him that he owns his clothes, his furniture, his toys, means nothing to him. Though he uses them he does not know why or how they are his. He must be taken back to the origin of property.

The easiest way for him to learn about property is through the work he does in the garden in imitation of the gardener. He plants beans and when they come up they 'belong' to him. To explain what that term means I make him feel that he has put his time, his work, his effort, himself into them. Then one day he finds his beans dug up by Robert the gardener. The ground 'belongs' to the gardener and he must come to an arrangement with the man before he can raise beans again. The destructive child has to learn his lesson in another way. He breaks the windows of his room, Let the wind blow on him night and day and do not worry about him catching cold. It is better for him to catch cold than to be a fool. If he goes on breaking windows shut him up in a dark room without windows. The time will come when he has learned what property means and he is willing to respect other people's belongings.

We are now in the moral world and the door is open to vice. With conventions and duties come deceit and lying. As soon as we can do what we ought not to do, we seek to hide our misdeeds. With the failure to prevent evil-doing the question of punishment arises. On fact there is never any need to inflict punishment as such on children. It should always come to them as the natural consequence of their bad conduct. In the case of lying, for example, you need not punish them because they have lied, but so arrange that if they lie they will not be believed even when they speak the truth, and will be accused of bad things they have not done.

Actually children's lies are all the work of their teachers. They try to teach them to tell the truth and in doing so teach them to lie. As for those of us who only give our pupils lessons of a practical kind and prefer them to be good rather than clever, we never demand the truth from them for fear they should hide it, and we never exact any promise lest they be tempted to break it. If something wrong has been done in my absence and I do not know the culprit, I take care not to accuse Emile or to ask: 'Was it you?' Nothing could be more indiscreet than such a question, especially if the child is guilty.

If he thinks you know he has done wrong you will seem to be trying to trap him and the idea will turn him against you. If he thinks you do not know he will ask: 'Why should I reveal my fault?' and the imprudent question will be a temptation to lying.

What has been said about lying applies in many respects to all the other duties prescribed for children. To make them pious you take them to church where they are bored. You make them gabble prayers till they look forward to the happy time when they will no longer pray to God. You make them give alms to inspire charity, as if alms-giving were a matter for children only. Drop these pretences, teachers. Be virtuous and good yourselves, and the examples you set will impress themselves on your pupils' memories, and in due season will enter their hearts.

Negative Education: (2) No Verbal Learning

The apparent ease with which children learn is their misfortune. It is not seen that this very facility proves that they are learning nothing. Their smooth polished brain is like a mirror which throws back the objects presented to it. Nothing gets in, nothing remains behind. They remember words but ideas are reflected off. Those who listen to them understand what the words mean but they themselves do not.

Though memory and reasoning are essentially different faculties they depend on each other in their development. Before the age of reason the child receives images but not ideas. The difference between them is that images are simply the exact pictures of sense-given objects, whereas ideas are notions of the objects determined by their relations. An image may exist by itself in the imagining mind, but every idea presupposes other ideas. Imagination is just seeing, but conception implies comparison. Our sensations are purely passive, different from our perceptions or ideas which are the outcome of an active principle of judgment.

That is why I say that children being incapable of judgment have no true memory. They retain sounds, shapes, sensations, but rarely ideas, and still more rarely their relations. It may be objected that they learn some of the elements of geometry, but really that only shows that so far from being able to reason for themselves they cannot even recollect the reasoning of others. For if you follow these little geometricians in their lesson you will find that all they have recollected is the exact picture of the figure and the words of the demonstration. The least new question upsets them and so does any change of figure. Their knowledge is all in sensation; nothing has got through to the understanding. Their memory itself is scarcely any more perfect than the other faculties since they nearly always have to re-learn the things whose names they learned in childhood when they grow up. Nevertheless I am far from thinking that children have no kind of reasoning. On the contrary, I notice that they think very well on everything which bears on their present and obvious interest. Where people go wrong is in regard to the things they actually know. They credit them with knowledge they do not possess, and make them reason about things beyond their comprehension.

The professional pedagogues speak differently, but it is evident from their own performance that they think exactly as I do. For what in fact do they teach? Nothing but words. Among the various sciences they boast of teaching their pupils, they take good care not to include those which are really useful, because these would be the sciences dealing with facts, in which the children's failure would be evident. They choose subjects like heraldry, geography, chronology and the languages in which acquaintance with terms gives the appearance of knowledge: studies so remote from men and especially from children that it would be surprising if ever they came to be of use even once in a lifetime.

Languages. It may seem strange that I reckon the study of languages among the futilities of education, but it must be remembered that I am only speaking now about the studies of the early years; and whatever may be said I do not believe that, apart from prodigies, any child under twelve or fifteen has ever really learned two languages. I agree that if the study of language was merely one of words it would be quite proper for children, but with the change in symbols the ideas represented are also modified. It is only the thought that is common: the spirit in each language has its own distinctive form. Of these different forms the child has only the one he uses, and he is limited to it till the age of reason. To have two languages he would have to be able to compare ideas, and how can he compare ideas he can barely conceive? He can then learn only a single language. But, you will tell me, some pupils learn several languages. I deny that. I have seen little prodigies who were supposed to speak five or six languages. I have heard them speak German, then use Latin, French and Italian in succession. Actually they made use of five or six different vocabularies, but in every case it was German they were speaking. The words were changed, but not the language.

To conceal their own incapacity teachers prefer the dead languages in which there are no longer any judges to call them in question. The familiar use of these languages has been lost a long time ago and we have to be content to imitate the language found in books. That is what is called 'speaking the language'. If the teachers' Latin and Greek are like that, judge what the children's are like.

Geography. In any study whatever, the representing symbols mean nothing apart from the idea of the things represented. But children are always limited to symbols. The teacher thinks he is giving them a description of the earth in geography, but actually he is only giving them a knowledge of maps. He tells them the names of towns, countries, rivers, but the children have no notion that they exist anywhere but on the paper shown to them. I remember seeing somewhere a geography which began: 'What is the world? It is a cardboard globe.' There you have the child's geography. I maintain in fact that after two years of the sphere and cosmography, there is not a ten-year-old child who could find his way from Paris to St. Denis by the rules he has been taught. These are the learned doctors who know just where Pekin, Ispahan, Mexico and all the countries of the world are.

History. It is still more ridiculous to set children to study history. History is supposed to be a collection of facts within their comprehension. But what is meant by 'facts'? Is it credible that the relations determining historical facts should be so easy to grasp that the ideas of them should readily take shape in children's minds? Or that there can be a real knowledge of events without a knowledge of their causes and their effects? If history is no more than an account of human actions in purely physical terms there is absolutely nothing to be learned from it. Try to make children appreciate these actions in terms of moral relations and you will see then whether they are old enough to learn history.

It is easy to put into their mouths words like 'king',

'empire', 'war', 'conquest', 'revolution', 'law,' but when it comes to a question of attaching precise ideas to such words, the explanations will be very different from those Emile got in his dealings with Robert the gardener.

Even if there is no book study the kind of memory the child has does not remain idle. All that he sees and hears makes its impression on him and he remembers it. He keeps a record in himself of the deeds and words of people. The world around him is the book in which without knowing it he is continually adding to the stores of memory, against the time when his judgment can profit by them. It is in the choice of these objects and in the constant care taken to put before him the things he can know and hide from him the things he ought not to know that the art of memory training consists. This is what must be done to form a storehouse of the knowledge which is to serve for his education in youth and for his conduct all through life.

Fables. Emile will never learn anything by heart, not even fables like those of La Fontaine, simple and charming though they be; for the words of fables are no more fables than the words of history are history. How can people be so blind as to call fables the ethics of childhood and not realise that the moral which amuses also misleads? Fables may instruct men, but it is necessary to speak the naked truth to children. My contention is that the child does not understand the fables he is taught, for whatever you do to make them simple the instruction you want to draw from them implies ideas beyond his grasp.

In all La Fontaine's book of fables there are only five or six of childlike simplicity. The first and best of these is 'The Crow and the Fox'. Analyse it line by line and it will be evident how very unsuitable it is for children.

'*Mr. Crow, on a tree perched.*' Have the children seen a crow? Do they know what a crow is? Why 'Mr.'? The usual order of words would be: 'perched on a tree'. Why the inversion? '*Held in his beak a cheese.*' What kind of a cheese? Could a crow hold a cheese in its beak? There are difficulties in every line, not merely of understanding, but of morals. The fox flatters and lies to get the crow to drop the cheese. What conclusion will the child draw? Watch children learning their fables and you will see that the morals they draw are just the opposite of what they were intended to draw. They laugh at the crow but are fond of the fox.

Reading. When I get rid of all the usual tasks of children in this way I also get rid of the books which are the chief cause of unhappiness to them. Reading is the greatest plague of childhood. Emile at the age of twelve will scarcely know what a book is. But at least, I will be told, he must be able to read. I agree. He must be able to read when he needs to read. Before that it will only be a bother to him.

If nothing is to be exacted from children by way of obedience it follows that they will only learn what they feel to be of actual and present advantage, either because they like it, or because it is of use to them. Otherwise, what motive would they have for learning? The art of speaking to absent people and hearing from them, of communicating personally our sentiments and our wishes, is an art whose usefulness can be made obvious to people of all ages; but by some strange perversity it has become a torment for childhood. Why should this be? Because the children have been compelled to learn it against their will, and made to put it to purposes which mean nothing for them.

Great stress is laid on finding better methods of teaching

children to read. Reading cases and cards have been invented, and the child's room has been turned into a printer's shop. Locke suggested the use of dice. Fancy all this elaborate contrivance! A surer way that nobody thinks of is to create the desire to read. Give the child this desire and have done with gadgets and any method will be good.

Present interest: that is the great motive impulse, the only one that leads sure and far. Emile sometimes receives from his father or his friends letters inviting him to a dinner, a walk, a boating party, or some public entertainment. These notes are short, clear, precise and well written. He must find some one to read them for him. This person is either not to be found at the right moment or is no more disposed to be helpful to the boy than the boy was to him the night before. In this way the chance is lost. By the time the note is read the time is past. If only he could read himself! He receives more letters and does his best to read them; and finally deciphers half a letter, something about going out tomorrow to eat cream. But where? And with whom? How hard he tries to read the rest! I do not think Emile will have any need of reading devices. Shall I go on now to speak about writing? Oh no. I am ashamed to amuse myself with such trifles in an educational treatise.

The Training of the Body

If on the plan I have begun to outline, you follow rules the very opposite of those commonly accepted, and instead of directing your pupil's mind to other places and times you set yourself to keep his attention on what directly affects him, you will find him capable of perception, memory, and even reasoning. That is the order of nature.

As the sentient being becomes active he acquires increasing discernment with his growing powers. If then you want to cultivate intelligence in your pupil cultivate the powers he has to control. Exercise his body continually. Make him vigorous and healthy and he will turn wise and reasonable.

It is true that this method will make him stupid if you are always saying 'Come', 'Go', 'Do this', 'Don't do that'. Nevertheless it is a shocking blunder to imagine that physical exercise is injurious to the operations of the mind; as if the two kinds of activity did not proceed together, with mind always directing body. There are two sets of men, peasants and savages, whose bodies are in constant activity, neither of whom gives any thought to the cultivation of their minds. The peasants are coarse and clumsy; the savages are known for their keen senses and even more for the subtlety of their minds. Why the difference? The peasant is a creature of routine: he always does what he is told, or what he has seen his father do, or what he himself has done from childhood. Habit and obedience take the place of reason. It is a different matter with the savage. He is not attached to any one place, has no prescribed task, obeys no one, has no law but his own will, and is compelled to reason about every action in his life. The more his body is exercised the better his mind becomes. Strength and reason develop together and help each other.

Which of our pupils, I ask you, learned teacher, resembles the savage and which the peasant? Your pupil is always under authority and does nothing without instructions. What need is there for him to think when you do all his thinking for him? Seeing that you have undertaken to look after him he feels himself free from this care. He relies on your judgment. He does not need to foresee the coming of rain, because you study the sky for him. He does not need to time his walk: there is no chance that you will let him pass his dinner hour. You soften him physically by inaction, but that does not make his understanding more flexible. On the contrary, you end up by discrediting what reason he has by making him use it on things that are of little account to him. As for my pupil, or rather the pupil of nature, he has been trained from the beginning to depend on himself as much as possible and is not always running to other people. He exercises judgment and foresight, and reasons about everything that directly affects him. He does not know a word about what is going on in the world but he can do whatever he himself requires to do. Being continually active, he is compelled to observe many things and know their effects. He learns his lessons from nature and not from men. Body and mind work together as he acts on his own ideas. The stronger he makes himself the more judicious in action he grows.

Sense Training

The first natural movements of man result from his effort to cope with all that surrounds him and to investigate the sensory qualities in the various objects which concern himself. His first study therefore is a kind of experimental physics with self-preservation as its aim. This is the time to become acquainted with the sensory relations things have with us. Since everything that enters into the human understanding comes through the senses, the first reason of man is a reason of the senses. On this the intellectual reason is based. Our first masters of philosophy are our feet, our hands and our eyes. To put books in place of this experience does not teach us to reason: only to be credulous and to borrow the reason of others.

The senses are the first faculties to take form and mature in us. They should therefore be the first to be cultivated. They are generally the ones most neglected. To train them calls for more than the use of them. It means learning to judge properly by them: learning, one might say, to feel. We do not know how to touch, see or hear, until we have learned.

There is a purely natural activity which helps to make the body vigorous without bringing judgment into play: as in swimming, running, jumping, whipping a top, throwing stones. All these are very good for arms and legs, but surely we have eyes and ears which also come into play. Then do not limit training to the physical activities, but train all the senses that direct them. Get as much out of each one as possible and check the impression got from one sense by the others. Measure, count, weigh, compare. Do not employ force till you have calculated the resistance to be overcome. In every action let the calculation of the effect precede the use of the means. Teach the child never to make insufficient or unnecessary efforts. Suppose a mass has to be moved: if he takes a lever that is too long he will waste his strength on too much movement; if he takes one that is too short, he will not have enough force. Experience will teach him to choose a rod that is exactly right.

The Sense of Touch. Our senses are not all equally under our control. Touch is active throughout our waking hours. It is spread out over the whole surface of our bodies, always ready to warn us of anything likely to do us hurt. Thanks to this constant exercise it is the sense of which we have earliest experience and consequently it has least need of special cultivation. Nevertheless we observe that the blind have a surer and finer sense of touch than ourselves, because lacking sight they are compelled to derive from this first sense the judgments usually furnished by sight. Why then are we not trained to walk in the dark like them and recognise the things we touch? We are blind half our lives, with the difference that those who are really blind are always able to get about, while we dare not take a step at dead of night. We have lights, of course, but they are not always available. Personally I prefer Emile to have eyes at the end of his fingers. If you are shut up in a building in the middle of the night, clap your hands. From the resonances of the room you will perceive whether the space is great or small, and whether you are in the middle or in a corner. Stand in one spot and turn all round: if there is an open door a slight draught will tell you where it is. Such observations and a thousand like them can be best made at night when we are not aided or distracted by sight.

I advise plenty of night games. People are naturally scared by the night. This fear is commonly attributed to nurses' tales but that is a mistake. There is a natural cause: the same cause that makes deaf people suspicious and common folk superstitious—ignorance of what is going on around us. When I see nothing, I cannot help thinking that there are a thousand things all about me ready to do me harm, against which I am defenceless. All that might reassure me exists only in reason, and instinct speaks more strongly to the other effect. But the cause of the evil once found suggests the cure. Habit invariably conquers imagination. Do not reason therefore with anyone you want to cure of night terrors. Take him often into the darkness and you can be sure that this will do more good than all the arguments of the scientists.

Though touch is the sense in most constant use its judgments remain more vague and imperfect than any other. It acts in conjunction with sight, and since the eye reaches the object more quickly than the hand, the mind almost always makes its judgment without touch. On the other hand, the judgments of touch are the most sure just because they are the most limited and they serve to correct the blunders of the other senses. In the same way, touch may supplement hearing since sounds excite in sonorous bodies vibrations which can be felt by touch. By placing the hand on the body of a 'cello it is possible to distinguish without the help of eye or ear from the way the wood vibrates and quivers whether the sound that issues is deep or sharp, whether it is drawn from the treble or the bass string. I have no doubt that if our touch were trained to appreciate these differences we might come in time to hear a whole tune through the fingers. In that case it might be possible to speak to deaf people by means of music.

Sight. Sight with the widest range of all our senses is the most faulty. Though it far outstrips the rest, its operations are too speedy and too extensive to be corrected by them. For this reason we must follow a different method of training in the case of sight. Instead of simplifying the sensation, we must always check up on it by subjecting the visual organ to the tactile organ and restraining the impetuosity of sight by the slow orderly pace of touch. Unless we do so our guesswork measurements are bound to be very inexact. There is no precision in the glance of the eye by which we estimate heights, lengths, depths and distances; and the proof that the fault is not in the sense of sight but in the use we make of it, is to be found in the fact that engineers, surveyors, architects, builders and painters are generally surer in estimates by eye and more exact in measures of space than others. Their occupations give them an experience in this sphere which the rest of us fail to acquire.

There are many ways of interesting children in the measurement and estimation of distances. Here is a very high cherry tree. How shall we gather the cherries? Will the ladder in the barn be big enough? How are we to get across this wide stream? Will one of the planks in the courtyard reach from bank to bank? We want to fish in the moat from our windows. How many yards will our line need to be? I want to make a swing between these two trees. Will a rope of two fathoms be enough? I am told that our room in the new house is to be twenty-five feet square. Do you think it will suit us? Will it be bigger than this one? We are hungry. To which of the two nearby villages can we get most quickly for dinner?

Sight is the sense most closely linked with judgments of the mind. That is why learning to see is a lengthy process. It is only after we have compared sight and touch for a long time that sight gives a faithful report of shapes and distances. Without touch and movement the most piercing eyes in the world could not give us any idea of space. It is only by walking, touching, counting and measuring dimensions that we learn to estimate them; but on the other hand, if we were always measuring, the sense of sight would continue to rely on instruments and never acquire precision. I should like to have Emile's first estimates checked by actual measurements so that he may correct his mistakes and improve his seeing. The same natural measures are in use almost everywhere: a man's pace, the stretch of his arms, his height. When the child is measuring the height of the storey of a house his tutor may serve him as a measuring rod. If he is estimating the height of a steeple he can measure it by the houses. To determine the length of the road he can count the hours taken to walk along it. But let nobody do all this for him. He must do it himself.

To learn how to get an exact idea of the extent and size of bodies, we must become acquainted with their shapes and even copy them. At bottom this copying depends on the laws of perspective and it is impossible to guess size from appearance without some feeling for these laws. Children, who are born imitators, all try to draw. I want my pupil to cultivate the art, not so much for the art itself as for the exactness of eye and the dexterity of hand it produces. I will take good care therefore not to let him have a drawing master who only gives him copies to reproduce. I do not want him to have any teacher but nature, nor any models but objects. He must have the original thing before his eyes and not a paper representation. He must draw a house from a house, a tree from a tree, a man from a man, so as to get accustomed to the close observation of objects and their appearances.

I know well enough that for a long time he will make unrecognisable scrawls, and that he will be slow in attaining the elegant contours and the light touch of the draughtsman. Possibly also he may never come to appreciate picturesque effects, or acquire good taste in drawing. As against that he will certainly get a truer eye and a surer hand, and learn the right relations of size and figure in animals, plants and natural objects, with a readier sense of perspective. My intention is to have him know things and not merely copy them.

I have said that geometry is beyond the capacity of children, but that is the teacher's fault. We do not realise that their method is different from ours, and that what is for us an art of reasoning is for them an art of seeing. Instead of teaching them our method it would be better for us to employ theirs; for our way of learning geometry is much more a matter of imagination than of reasoning.

To find the proof for a proposition we have to imagine all the propositions already known from which it can be deduced and choose the one that is relevant. On this method the most exact reasoner may be baffled if he is not inventive. The consequence is that instead of making us find the proofs for ourselves, the teacher dictates them to us: instead of teaching us to reason he reasons for us and only exercises our memory. Make exact figures, combine them, put one on top of another, examine their relations. In this way you will discover the whole of elementary geometry as you proceed from observation to observation, without thought of definitions or problems or any form of proof but simple superimposition. As for me I make no pretence of teaching Emile geometry. He is to teach me. I will look for relations and get him to find them. For example, instead of using compasses to draw a circle I will draw it with a pencil at the end of a thread that turns round a pivot. After that, when I want to compare the radii, Emile will laugh at me and make me understand that with the thread drawn tight the distances from the centre cannot be unequal. If again I want to measure an angle of sixty degrees, I describe a complete circle from the vertex of the angle and I find that the part of the circle between the two sides of the angle is the sixth part of the circle. Then I draw a still larger circle with the same centre and find that the second arc is also a sixth of its circle. I go on drawing concentric circles until Emile, shocked at my stupidity, points out that every arc great or small contained by the same angle is always a sixth of its circle. We are now ready to use the protractor.

The exact drawing of geometrical figures is commonly neglected and the stress is laid on the proof. With us, on the contrary, the really important matter will be the drawing of lines which are quite straight, quite exact, quite equal, and to make perfect squares and circles. To verify the exactness of a figure we will examine its obvious properties. We will fold the two semi-circles along the diameter, and the two halves of the square along the diagonal. We will compare our two figures to see which of them has its edges fitting most precisely. We will discuss whether there is always this symmetry in parallelograms and other figures, and sometimes we will try to forecast the result of our experiments. For my pupil, geometry is simply the art of using rule and compass.

The Sense of Hearing. What has been said about the two senses of sight and touch may serve to exemplify the method of training the other senses. As we have compared sight with touch it is a good thing to compare it in the same way with hearing, and learn which of two impressions starting at the same time from a body first reaches its special sense organ. When the flash of a cannon is seen there is still time to take cover, but when the noise is heard the bullet has arrived. It is possible to judge the distance of thunder by the interval between flash and crash. See that the child makes acquaintance with all these phenomena, either by direct experience in the case of those within his reach, or by inference in the case of the others. But it would be much better for him to know nothing about them than be told by you.

In the voice we have an organ which corresponds with hearing. There is nothing like this in the case of sight. The sense of hearing can be cultivated by the joint exercise of the active and the passive organs.

Man has three kinds of voice: the speaking voice, the singing voice, and the expressive voice which serves as the language of the passions and gives life to song and speech. The child has the same three kinds of voice, but he cannot use them in combination. The three are best united in perfect music, but such music is beyond the powers of children and there is no soul in their singing, just as there is no expression in their speech. Our pupil's speech will be even more flat and simple, because his passions have been kept dormant. We must not give him, therefore, tragic or comic parts to play, or try to teach him what is called declamation. He will have too much sense to speak with special feeling about things he does not understand, or try to give expression to sentiments he has never experienced.

Teach him to speak plainly and clearly, to articulate well, to pronounce precisely and unaffectedly, to recognise and practise the proper accent and always to speak loud enough to be heard without speaking too loudly. The same principles apply in singing. Make his voice true, even, flexible, sonorous, and his ear responsive to time and harmony, but nothing more. Imitative and theatrical music is not suitable for him. I would even prefer him not to sing words; but if he wanted words to sing I would try to compose songs for him on his own level of interest and ideas.

As might be expected, I am no more anxious to have him learn to read music than to read writing. There is no hurry to fix his mind on conventional signs. This I admit seems to raise a difficulty. Even if the knowledge of notes does not appear to be more necessary for singing than a knowledge of letters for writing there is a difference between them. When we talk we are expressing our own ideas, whereas in singing we are for the most part expressing other people's. In the latter case we must read. But in the first instance hearing can take the place of reading: a song is registered more faithfully on the ear than on the eye. More than that, to know music well we must compose songs as well as sing them, and the two things must go together if we are ever to know music properly. First train your young musician in the making of regular phrases with well marked cadences; next get him to connect these phrases by a very simple modulation and then to indicate their different relations by a correct punctuation, through a fit choice of cadences and rests. Above all, avoid fantastic tunes and anything with pathos or forced expression. What is wanted in every case is a simple tuneful melody with the bass so clearly marked that he can feel and accompany it without difficulty. This means that for the training of voice and ear the child should always sing with the harpsichord.

The Sense of Taste. Among our various sensations we are usually affected most by those that come from taste. A thousand things are indifferent to touch, hearing and sight but almost nothing is indifferent to taste. Moreover, the activity of this sense is wholly physical and material: it is the only one that makes no appeal to the imagination. This might seem to make taste inferior to the other senses, and to render our inclination to yield to its attraction more base, but I draw the opposite conclusion —that the best way to manage children is by the appeal to the mouth. Greed as a motive is greatly to be preferred to vanity, since greed is a natural appetite directly connected with the senses, while vanity is the product of convention, subject to the caprice of men and open to all kinds of abuse. Greed is the passion of childhood, and has nothing to do with the other passions. When the child grows up it will be driven out by countless sentiments, unlike vanity which is stimulated by them and ends up by absorbing them all.

At the same time, I would not have an unwise use made of this lowly expedient nor have a dainty morsel preferred to the honour of doing a good deed. But childhood is, or ought to be, the age of games and frolics, and I do not see why purely physical exercises should not have material prizes. When a Young Majorcan sees a basket at the top of a tree and brings it down with his sling, is he not entitled to profit by it and restore the strength he has expended with a good dinner? A good meal should never be a reward, but there is no reason why it should not sometimes come as the result of efforts made to get it. Emile does not consider the cake I put on a stone as the prize for running well. All he knows is that the only way to get the cake is to reach the spot before anybody else.

However you bring up children, provided you accustom them to a simple diet, you can leave them to eat, run and play as they please, and can be sure that they will never eat too much and never suffer from indigestion. But if you keep them hungry half the time and they can find ways of escaping from your vigilance, they will make up for it by eating gluttonously till they can eat no more. Appetite is only immoderate because we try to impose on it other rules than those of nature. Among peasants the bread bin and the fruit closet are always open, and neither children nor adults ever have indigestion.

The Sense of Smell. The sense of smell is to taste what sight is to touch. It goes before it, and gives warning of how it is likely to be affected by different substances. I have been told that savages have not the same reaction to smells as we have, and judge quite differently regarding good and bad odours. I can quite believe it. Odours by themselves are feeble sensations. They stir the imagination more than the senses, and affect us by the thoughts they call up rather than by direct impression. That is why the sense of smell should not be very active in childhood,

In the early years the imagination, being little moved as yet by the passions, is scarcely affected by emotion, and the experience which enables us to foresee with one sense what another sense promises is still lacking. Not that the sensation is less delicate in children than in men—it may even be more delicate—but that, in the absence of any other ideas, they are not so readily affected by feelings of pleasure or pain. I have the notion that if children were trained to scent their dinner as a dog scents game, it might be possible to bring their sense of smell to the same perfection. But I do not really see that any special use can be made of this sense unless to make the children appreciate its natural relations with that of taste.

Emile at the Age of Twelve

Assuming that my method is that of nature and that I have not made any mistakes in putting it into practice, I have now brought my pupil through the land of the sensations right up to the bounds of childish reason. The first step beyond this should take him towards manhood. But before entering on this new stage let us cast our eyes backward for a moment on the one we have traversed. Each age and state of life has its own proper perfection, its own distinctive maturity. People sometimes speak about a complete man. Let us think rather of a complete child. This vision will be new for us and perhaps not less agreeable.

When I picture to myself a boy of ten or twelve, healthy, strong and well built for his age, only pleasant thoughts arise in me, whether for his present or for his future. I see him bright, eager, vigorous, care-free, completely absorbed in the present, rejoicing in abounding vitality. I see him in the years ahead using senses, mind and power, as they develop from day to day. I view him as a child and he pleases me. I think of him as a man and he pleases me still more. His warm blood seems to heat my own. I feel as if I were living in his life and am rejuvenated by his vivacity.

The clock strikes and all is changed. In an instant his eye grows dull and his merriment disappears. No more mirth, no more games! A severe, hard-faced man takes him by the hand, says gravely, 'Come away, sir', and leads him off. In the room they enter I get a glimpse of books. Books! What a cheerless equipment for his age. As he is dragged away in silence, he casts a regretful look around him. His eyes are swollen with tears he dare not shed, his heart heavy with sighs he dare not utter.

Come, my happy pupil, and console us for the departure of the wretched boy. Here comes Emile, and at his approach I have a thrill of joy in which I see he shares. It is his friend and comrade, the companion of his games to whom he comes. His person, his bearing, his countenance reveal assurance and contentment. Health glows in his face. His firm step gives him an air of vigour. His complexion is refined without being effeminate; sun and wind have put on it the honourable imprint of his sex. His eyes are still unlighted by the fires of sentiment and have all their native serenity. His manner is open and free without the least insolence or vanity.

His ideas are limited but precise. If he knows nothing by heart, he knows a great deal by experience. If he is not as good a reader in books as other children, he reads better in the book of nature. His mind is not in his tongue but in his head. He has less memory but more judgment. He only knows one language, but he understands what he says; and if he does not talk as well as other children he can do things better than they can.

Habit, routine and custom mean nothing to him. What he did yesterday has no effect on what he does today. He never follows a fixed rule and never accepts authority or example. He only does or says what seems good to himself. For this reason you must not expect stock speeches or studied manners from him but just the faithful expression of his ideas and the conduct that comes from his inclinations.

You will find in him a few moral notions relating to his own situation, but not being an active member of society he has none relating to manhood. Talk to him about liberty, property and even convention, and he may understand you thus far. But speak to him about duty and obedience, and he will not know what you mean. Command him to do something, and he will pay no heed. But say to him: 'If you will do me this favour, I will do the same for you another time'; and immediately he will hasten to oblige. For his part, if he needs any help he will ask the first person he meets as a matter of course. If you grant his request he will not thank you, but will feel that he has contracted a debt. If you refuse, he will neither complain nor insist. He will only say: 'It could not be done'. He does not rebel against necessity once he recognises it.

Work and play are all the same to him. His games are his occupations: he is not aware of any difference. He goes into everything he does with a pleasing interest and freedom. It is indeed a charming spectacle to see a nice boy of this age with open smiling countenance, doing the most serious things in his play or profoundly occupied with the most frivolous amusements.

Emile has lived a child's life and has arrived at the maturity of childhood, without any sacrifice of happiness in the achievement of his own perfection. He has acquired all the reason possible for his age, and in doing so has been as free and as happy as his nature allowed him to be. If by chance the fatal scythe were to cut down the flower of our hopes we would not have to bewail at the same time his life and his death, nor add to our griefs the memory of those we caused him. We would say that at any rate he had enjoyed his childhood and that nothing we had done had deprived him of what nature gave.

BOOK THREE

THE APPROACH OF ADOLESCENCE

Editorial Note

The years just after twelve, according to Rousseau, still belong to the period of childhood. The boy has not yet passed the dividing line of puberty. But a change has come with a fresh accession of physical strength. For the first time in life his powers are more than enough for the demands made on them, and the urge to activity, which up to this time has found ample expression in bodily action, now takes mental form. There is a greater capacity for sustained attention. His thinking is still concerned with the sense-given facts but he is no longer confined to what is immediately presented to his senses. He can keep more than one thing at a time in mind, and can even compare and reason about the phenomena within his experience. In consequence he can look forward into the future and can exercise foresight. He still lacks aesthetic and moral insight and has only a rudimentary understanding of social relations. But he can now appreciate the *use* of things and hence is able to understand how men in society can be mutually helpful on the basis of a division of labour. He sees also why he himself must work. Work means for him doing what he does not want to do, in order to prevent a greater evil later on.

The social ideal that corresponds with this new understanding is embodied in the story of Robinson Crusoe, the solitary, self-sufficient man who uses his intelligence to find for himself and by himself practical solutions for the problems of his island life as they occur. Emile's island is the world. He applies himself to the scientific exploration of it, and finds a use for the sciences he has learned when he becomes a workman with a basic skill which is applicable in all the different crafts. He has now begun to study seriously, and science and handicraft are his two main concerns. Because of his mental limitations, art, history, literature, social science and religion are still in the future for him.

The Third Stage of Childhood

The whole course of life up to adolescence is a time of weakness, but there is one point during this first age of man at which strength exceeds the demands made on it by needs, and the growing creature though still absolutely weak becomes relatively strong. With needs incompletely developed, his powers more than suffice. As a man he would be very feeble: as a child he is very strong. This is the third stage of early life which for lack of a better word I continue to call childhood. It is not yet the age of puberty, but adolescence draws near.

At twelve or thirteen the child's powers develop much more rapidly than his needs. The sex passions, the most violent and terrible of all, have not yet awakened. He is indifferent to the rigours of weather and seasons, and braves them light-heartedly. His growing body heat takes the place of clothing. Appetite is his sauce, and everything nourishing tastes good. When he is tired he stretches himself out on the ground and goes to sleep. He is not troubled by imaginary wants. What people think does not trouble him. Not only is he self-sufficient but his strength goes beyond his requirements. It is the most precious time in life, and it comes but once. Being very short, it is all the more important for him to make good use of it. It is the time for labour, for instruction, for studies. That is what nature herself indicates.

Human intelligence has its limits. Not only is it impossible for anyone to know everything. It is not even possible to master the little that other people know. Choice must therefore be made of the things to be learned as well as of the time best suited for learning them. Of the knowledge at our disposal, some is false, some useless and some but serves to engender pride in its possession. Only the small part of it that contributes to our well-being is worthy of study by a wise man and consequently by the child we want to become wise. It is not a question of knowing things, but of knowing what is useful. And from this must be omitted in the case of the child those truths about human relations which require for their comprehension a fully developed understanding.

Note how with the consideration of what is useful, we are gradually approaching moral notions involving the distinction of good and evil. Up to this point in the child's education we have only recognised the law of necessity. Now we must have regard for utility. Soon we will be coming to what is fitting and good.

It is the same instinct that animates the different human faculties. To the activity of the body with its urge to growth succeeds the activity of the mind eager to learn. Children begin by being restless; then they become curious; and this curiosity when rightly directed becomes the driving power of the age we have now reached. Always distinguish between the urges that come from nature and those due to a regard for what people think. There is a quest for knowledge which comes only from the desire for reputation as a scholar: another which springs from natural curiosity about anything interesting, near and far. The innate desire for happiness and the impossibility of finding complete satisfaction for it prompt an unceasing search for new sources of interest. Such is the basic principle of curiosity, a principle natural to the human heart but dependent for the measure of its development on our passions and our intelligence. If a scientist were marooned on a desert island with his apparatus and his books, and knew that he would have to pass the rest of his life alone, he would concern himself little further about the physical universe, the laws of attraction, or the differential calculus. He would probably never open a single book, but he would go on exploring his island to its remotest corner.

The Scientific Studies of Emile

The island of the human race is the earth: the most striking object that meets our eyes is the sun. As soon as we get away from ourselves, our first observations inevitably fall on one or other of these.

What a jump, it will perhaps be said. Only a short time ago we were wholly taken up with our immediate surroundings; and here we are, all at once, traversing the earth and reaching out to the bounds of the universe. The change has come with the development of powers and the new direction taken by the mind. In the state of weakness and insufficiency the task of self-preservation makes us concentrate on ourselves. With the coming of strength and power, the desire for a fuller life carries us as far afield as we can reach. But with the intellectual world still unknown, our thought goes no further than our eyes, and our understanding does not extend beyond the space it compasses.

Let us transform our sensations into ideas, but do not let us leap from objects of the senses to objects of the intellect. It is through the senses that we come to the intellect. The senses must always be our guides in the first operations of mind. The world must be our one book, facts the only instruction. The child who reads does not think: he only reads. He learns nothing but words.

Make your pupil attend to the phenomena of nature, and you will soon arouse his curiosity. But to nourish this curiosity, be in no hurry to satisfy it. Suggest problems but leave the solving of them to him. Whatever he knows, he should know not because you have told him, but because he has grasped it himself. Do not teach him science: let him discover it. If ever you substitute authority for reason in his mind, he will stop reasoning, and become the victim of other people's opinions.

To teach this child geography you set out to look for globes, spheres and maps. Why all these contrivances? Instead of these representations, begin by showing him the real thing, and let him know at least what you are talking about.

One fine evening we go for a walk in a suitable place where the open horizon allows a full view of the setting sun, and we note by landmarks the place of its setting. Next day, before the sun rises, we come back for a breath of air to the same spot. We see its coming heralded by streaks of light. The glow increases. The east seems all aflame. Every moment we expect to see it appear. At last we see it. The veil of darkness vanishes and the world appears in all its beauty. During the night the verdure has acquired a new vigour. The dawning day with its first golden beams reveals it covered with a glittering network of dew. The birds join in chorus to salute the Father of life. All these things in concourse bring to the senses an impression of freshness that seems to get right into the soul. There is a brief, heartfelt half-hour of enchantment.

Full of his own enthusiasm the teacher seeks to communicate it to the child. He expects to stir him by calling his attention to the sensations which have stirred himself.

This is just stupidity on his part. The life of the spectacle of nature is in man's heart: it must be felt to be seen. The child perceives the objects, but cannot perceive the relations that bind them, or hear the sweet harmony of their concord. It calls for an experience he has not acquired and sentiments beyond his range to get the impression resulting from these sensations as a whole.

Never talk to the child about things he cannot understand. Avoid descriptions, rhapsodies, figures of speech, poetry. The time has not yet come for sentiment and taste. Continue to be clear, direct, unemotional. Only too soon will a different language be necessary.

Be content to show him things at the right moment. Then when you see his curiosity sufficiently active, ask him some brief questions that will set him searching for an answer. On this particular occasion, after you and he have contemplated the rising sun, and you have called his attention to the mountains and adjacent objects and have let him talk freely about what he sees, you keep silence for some moments like a man in a dream, then remark: 'I think the sun set over there last night and rose here this morning. I wonder how that can be?' No more than that. If he asks questions make no reply. Speak about something else. If you leave him to himself, you can be sure he will think about it.

To be thoroughly convinced of some sense-given truth a child needs to puzzle over it for days before making his discovery. If he cannot grasp it properly, the way to make it more evident is to reverse the question. He may not know how the sun gets from where it sets to where it rises, but at any rate he knows how it gets from its rising to its setting. His own eyes tell him that. Unless your pupil is absolutely stupid, the analogy is too obvious for him to miss. Now he has got his first lesson in cosmography.

Since we always move on slowly from sensory idea to sensory idea, dwelling for a considerable time on the same idea and never forcing our pupil's attention, it is a long way from this first lesson to a knowledge of the sun's course, or the shape of the earth. But since the apparent movements of the heavenly bodies all proceed on the same principle and the first observation leads on to all the rest, less effort but more time is required to pass from the earth's rotation to the calculation of eclipses than to understand the succession of day and night.

There is some debate on whether the analytic or the synthetic method should be followed in the study of the sciences, but the choice is not always necessary. In some cases it is possible to break up the facts and to bring them together again in the same investigation, and to guide the child by this method of instruction when he seems to himself to be concerned with details. When the two processes can be combined in this fashion they serve to confim each other. Setting out from two opposite points without realising that they are going the same road, the boy will be very pleasantly surprised to find them converging. I should like, by way of example, to come to geography from opposite sides and combine the study of the earth's revolutions with the survey of its parts, beginning with the place where he lives. While the child is studying the sphere and being transported to the skies, bring him back to the regions of the earth and show him first of all his own home.

His two starting points will be his home town and his father's country house: then will come the places between the two and the nearby rivers; and finally the observation of the sun's position, to enable him to get his directions. This last is where the different facts meet.

He should make a map of it all for himself: a very simple map, with only two objects marked on it to begin with, to which he will gradually add the others as he comes to know them and determine their position and their distance. You can see already the advantage we have gained by putting a compass in his eyes.

Nevertheless, it will probably be necessary to give him a little guidance. But let it be very little, and avoid the appearance of it. If he goes wrong, do not correct his errors. Say nothing till he sees them and corrects them himself; or at most, arrange some practical situation which will make him realise things personally. If he never made mistakes he would never learn properly. In any case, the important thing is not that he should know the topography of the country, but that he should be able to get his information for himself. It does not matter greatly whether he has maps in his head, provided he knows what they represent and has a clear idea of the art of their construction.

The essential principle in my method is not to teach the child a great many things but to allow him to form only clear, exact ideas. It would not matter greatly if he knew nothing so long as he did not go wrong in his thinking. I only put truths into his head to save him from the errors he might learn instead. Reason and judgment are slow to come, but prejudices crowd in; and it is necessary to protect him from them.

During the first period of life time was plentiful. We only sought to have it occupied in any way at all to prevent it being put to a bad use. Now it is just the opposite, and we have not enough time to get all done that is useful. Bear in mind that the passions are near at hand, and that as soon as they knock at the door your pupil will no longer attend to anything else. The quiet period of intellect passes so rapidly and has so many other necessary occupations that it is folly to try to make the child a scholar within its span. It is not a question of teaching him the sciences, but of giving him a taste for them, and methods of acquiring them when this taste is better developed. This is most certainly a fundamental principle in all good education.

There is a connected system of general truths by which all the sciences are derived from common principles and are developed in succession. This is the philosophical method, but it is not the one we are concerned with here. Our method is quite different. It is particular objects which are associated with each other, and one leads on to the next. This order which holds the attention by a never-failing curiosity is the one followed by most men, and is the right order for children.

The method finds illustration in the way that Emile learns about the use of the compass in order to find direction in his map making. Tutor and pupil had already remarked on the properties of amber, glass and wax when rubbed, and from that went on to play with the magnet. One day shortly after, they pay a visit to a fair where they see a conjurer making a wax duck in a basin of water follow a piece of bread in which was concealed a magnet. In the end they construct a similar contrivance, which serves its purpose by leading them to observe that the duck with the magnet inside always comes to rest in the north-south direction. They have discovered the compass, or something that will serve the same purpose; and what is more important, they have made a beginning with the study of physics.

The earth has different zones and these zones have different temperatures. The seasonal changes become more evident the nearer we come to the pole. All bodies contract with cold and expand with heat. This effect is most easily measured in the case of liquids, and most obvious with alcohol: so we get the thermometer. The wind beats on the face: the air, therefore, is a fluid substance, which can be felt though it is not seen. If a glass is inverted in water, the water will not fill it unless there is an outlet for the air in it: the air, therefore, is capable of resistance. Plunge the glass down further, and the water will rise in the air space, but will not be able to fill it completely: the air, therefore, can be compressed to a certain extent. A ball full of compressed air bounces better than when it is filled with anything else: air, therefore, is an elastic substance. When lying in your bath raise your arm horizontally out of the water and you will feel it a tremendous weight: air, therefore, is heavy. By balancing air against other liquids its weight can be measured: hence the barometer, the siphon, the air-gun and the air-pump. All the laws of statics and hydrostatics can be discovered by experiments as rough and ready as these. I do not wish my pupil to go into a laboratory with its array of apparatus. The scientific atmosphere kills science.

I mean us to make all our equipment for ourselves, and I do not wish to begin by making apparatus. What I plan is that after we have got some notion of an experiment, seemingly by chance, we should gradually invent the instrument for its verification. I would rather not have our instruments so very precise, but have instead clear ideas about what they should be, and the results to be got from them. For my first physics lesson I do not go to look for a balance. I put a stick across the back of a chair, measure the length of the two parts of the stick when it balances, add equal or unequal weights to one end or the other, draw and push the stick as required, and end up with the discovery that equilibrium results from a reciprocal proportion between the amount of the weights and the length of the levers. In this way my young physicist is able to adjust balances even before he has seen one.

The most obvious advantage of these slow laborious investigations is that in the midst of speculative studies the body is kept active, and the hands trained for the useful work of mankind. The many instruments invented to help in experimentation and to make the senses more precise lead us to neglect the senses themselves. The more ingenious our tools, the coarser and clumsier our organs become. With all the instruments we gather around us we no longer make use of those we ourselves possess.

But when we apply to the construction of our instruments the skill which has taken their place, we add art to nature and become more ingenious without becoming any less skilful. If instead of keeping a child at his books I keep him busy in a workshop, his hands labour to the benefit of his mind. He becomes a man of science, but thinks himself only a workman.

I have already said that purely speculative knowledge is little suited for children, even in the pre-adolescent period. Without going very far into systematic physics, however, you should make sure that their experiments are linked together by some sort of deduction, so that with the help of this connection they may arrange them in order in their minds, and be able to recall them at need. It is very difficult to remember detached facts, and even reasonings for any length of time unless there is something to recall them.

In the search for the laws of nature, always begin with the commonest and most obvious phenomena, and accustom your pupil to consider such phenomena as facts and not as explanations. I take a stone and pretend to lay it in the air. I open my hand and the stone falls. I see Emile interested in what I am doing and I say: 'Why has this stone fallen?' What child will hold back at this question? Not one. Not even Emile. They will all say that the stone falls because it is heavy. 'And what do you mean by a thing being heavy,' I ask. Something that falls. The stone falls then because it falls. Here my young scientist comes to a dead stop. He has had his first lesson in systematic physics.

The Principle of Utility

With the child's advance in intelligence other considerations compel greater care in the choice of his occupations. As soon as he comes to know himself well enough to understand what constitutes happiness for him and can judge what is fitting and what is not, he is in a position to appreciate the difference between work and play, and to regard play as relaxation from work. Thereafter matters of real utility may enter into his studies and lead him to apply himself more diligently than he did to mere amusements. The law of necessity, always operative, soon teaches man to do what he does not like, in order to avoid evils he would like still less. Such is the practice of foresight; and from foresight, well or ill directed, comes all the wisdom or all the unhappiness of mankind.

When children foresee their needs their intelligence has made real progress. They begin to know the value of time. For this reason, it is important to accustom them to employ their time on objects of an obvious utility that are within their understanding. All that pertains to the moral order and to social usage should not be put before them yet, because it does not mean anything for them. Why do you want to set a child to the studies of an age he may never reach, to the detriment of studies suited for the present? But you will ask: 'Will there be time for him to learn what he ought to know when the occasion for its use arises?' That I do not know. What I do know is that it is impossible for him to learn it sooner. Our real teachers are experience and feeling, and no one ever appreciates what is proper to manhood till he enters into its situations. A child knows that he is destined to become a man. Such of the ideas of adult life as are within his comprehension are occasions of instruction for him, but he ought to be kept in absolute ignorance of all the rest. This whole book is one long demonstration of this educational principle.

As soon as we have managed to give our pupil some idea of what the word 'utility' means, we have another strong hold on him. This word makes a deep impression on him, provided it has meaning for him on his own age level and he can see its bearing on his present well being. 'What is the good of that?' Henceforth this is the sacred question, the decisive question between him and me, in all the situations of our life. This is my infallible response to all his questions, and it serves to check the multitude of foolish queries with which children constantly bother people. Note what a powerful instrument I am putting into your hands for dealing with your pupil. Since he does not know the reason of anything, you can reduce him to silence at will while you with your knowledge and experience can show him the use of all you put before him. But make no mistake about it: when you ask him this question you are teaching him to put it to you in his turn. You can be sure that in future he will never fail to ask about anything you tell him: 'What is the good of it?'

I do not like explanatory speeches. Young people pay
little attention to them and rarely remember them. Give
them facts. I cannot say often enough, that we allow too
great power to words. With our babbling education we
only make babblers.

Suppose, when I am studying with my pupil the course
of the sun and how to find our direction, he suddenly
stops me to ask what good purpose all this serves. What
a fine discourse I could give him—especially if people
were listening in to our conversation—about the use of
travel, the advantages of commerce, the special products
of different regions, the customs of different peoples, the
use of the calendar, the reckoning of the seasons for
agriculture, the art of navigation. Politics, natural
history, astronomy, even ethics and the law of nations,
might enter into my explanation so as to give my pupil
a great idea of all these subjects and a great desire to
learn them. But not a single idea of all this would the
boy understand. Unless he feared that he would be
bothering me, he would ask what was the use of taking
one's bearings. Actually our Emile, brought up in the
country and accustomed to get ideas the hard way,
would not listen to a single word of all this. At the first
sentence he did not understand he would run off and
leave me to perorate by myself. We must look for a more
ordinary solution. My display of science is of no use to
him.

When Emile wants to learn what use it is to know the
position of the forest north of Montmorency, I put him
off and next morning take him for a walk before breakfast.
We get lost and the more we wander the more tired and
hungry we become. We sit down to consider how we can
get out. Crying is no use. 'Let us see your watch. What
time is it?' 'It is noon,' says Emile, 'and I am so hungry.'

At twelve o'clock the day before, he is reminded, we were observing the position of the forest from Montmorency. 'Did we not say that the forest was . . .?' 'North of Montmorency,' says Emile, 'So Montmorency lies . . .' 'South of the forest.' But we know how to find the north at midday. 'Yes,' says Emile, 'by the direction of the shadows,' and comes to the conclusion that if we go the opposite way from the shadows we will find the town. And this we do. It is evident that astronomy is of some use after all.

The Game of Robinson Crusoe

I hate books. They only teach us to talk about what we do not know. It is said that Hermes engraved the elements of science on pillars for fear his discoveries might perish in a deluge. If he had impressed them firmly on the human brain, they would have been kept safe there by tradition.

Is there no way of bringing together all the lessons scattered through a multitude of books and grouping them together round some common object which, even at this age, might be easy to see, interesting to follow and thought-provoking? If it were possible to invent a situation in which all the natural needs of mankind were made obvious to the mind of a child, and the ways of providing for these needs made equally clear, the simple lifelike picture of this condition of things would give the child's imagination its first training.

Eager philosopher, I see your own imagination lighting up. Do not trouble yourself. This situation has been found, and with all respect to you has been described better than you could do it, at any rate with greater truth and simplicity. Since it is essential that there should be books, there happens to be one book which in my opinion furnishes the most satisfactory treatise on natural education. This is the first book my Emile will read. For a long time it will constitute his entire library, and will always occupy an honoured place in it. It will be the text on which all our talks on the natural sciences will form a commentary. It will serve as a touchstone for our judgment as we progress, and so long as our taste remains unspoiled, it will continue to give us pleasure. What is this marvellous book? Is it Aristotle? Or Pliny? Or Buffon? Oh no, it is *Robinson Crusoe*.

Robinson Crusoe alone on his island, without the help of his fellows and the tools of the various arts, yet managing to procure food and safety, and even a measure of well-being: here is something of interest for every age, capable of being made attractive to children in a thousand ways. This condition, I admit, is not that of social man, and probably it is not to be that of Emile, but he should use it in the evaluation of all other conditions. The surest way for him to rise above prejudices and to bring his own judgments into line with the true relations of things is to put himself at the point of view of a solitary man, and to judge everything as this man would with reference to its real utility.

Rid of all its lumber, this novel, beginning with the shipwreck of Robinson near his island and concluding with the arrival of the ship that is to take him away, will furnish Emile with both amusement and instruction during the period of life under consideration. I want his head to be turned by it, and to have him busy himself unceasingly with his castle, his goats and his plantations. I want him to learn, not from books but from experience, all the things he would need to know in such a situation. I want him to think he is Robinson and imagine himself clothed in skins, with a large hat, a large sabre and all the grotesque equipment of the character, even to the umbrella he will not need. I want him to be concerned about the measures he would take if any one thing happened to be lacking, scrutinising his hero's conduct to see whether anything has been omitted or could be done better. You may be sure that he will plan a house for himself like Crusoe's. This is the veritable castle in Spain of this blessed age, when all that is required for happiness is freedom and the necessaries of life.

What an opportunity there is in this phantasy for a skilful grown-up who knows how to awaken it and use it to advantage. The child, eager to build a storehouse for his island will be more zealous to learn than the master to teach. He will concentrate on everything that is of use for the purpose. You will no longer have to direct him, only to hold him back. For the rest, let us hasten to establish him on this island while he is able to find complete happiness on it, for the day draws near when he will no longer want to live alone, and when Friday's company will not content him.

The Choice of a Trade

The practice of the natural arts for which a single man is sufficient leads to the pursuit of the industrial arts which call for the co-operation of many hands. The former can be practised by solitaries and savages, but the latter can only come into being in the society which they make necessary. So long as there is only physical need each man is self-sufficient. It is the introduction of luxuries that makes the sharing and differentiation of labour essential.

Your main endeavour should be to keep away from

your pupil all the notions of social relations which are beyond his comprehension; but when the inter-relation of knowledge forces you to show him the mutual dependence of men, avoid the moral aspects and direct his attention to industry and the mechanical arts which make them useful to each other. As you take him from one workshop to another, never let him see any kind of work without putting his hand to it, and never let him leave till be knows perfectly the reason for all that he has observed. With that in view, set him an example by working yourself in the different occupations. To make him a master become an apprentice. You can be sure that he will learn more from an hour's work than he would remember after a day's explanations.

The value popularly attached to the different arts is in inverse ratio to their usefulness. The most useful arts are the worst paid, because the work necessary for everybody must be kept at a price within the reach of the poor. On the other hand, those important people who are called not artisans but artists work for the idle rich and put an arbitrary price on their baubles. My opinion is that in all cases the art which is most generally useful and most indispensable is the one which should be most highly regarded. The art which needs least help from the other arts is more entitled to esteem than those dependent on others. The first and most honourable of all the arts is agriculture. The forge comes second, carpentry third and the rest after. That is precisely how the child who has not been seduced by vulgar prejudices will judge them. Our Emile, thinking about the furnishing of his island, will draw important conclusions in these matters from his Robinson.

Reader, do not give too much thought to the bodily activity and the skill of hand of our pupil. Consider rather the direction we are giving to his childish curiosities. Consider his senses, his inventive mind, his foresight. Consider the good head he will have. He will want to know all about everything he sees and does, and will take nothing for granted. He will refuse to learn anything until he acquires the knowledge that is implied in it. When he sees a spring made he will want to know how the steel was got from the mine. If he sees the pieces of a box put together, he will want to know how the tree was cut. When he is using a tool himself he will not fail to say of the tool he uses: 'If I did not have this tool, how would I make one like it, or manage without it?'

At the beginning of this period of life we have taken advantage of the fact that our strength greatly exceeds our needs, to get away beyond ourselves. We have soared into the heavens and have surveyed the earth. We have studied the laws of nature. In a word, we have traversed the whole of our island. Now we come back gradually to our own dwelling. What is there for us to do when we have completed the study of our surroundings? We must convert them as much as we can to our own purposes. Up to this point, we have provided ourselves with all kinds of instruments without knowing which of them we will need. It may be that those which are of no use to us may be of service to other people and that we in turn may need theirs. In this way we will all find ourselves gaining by these exchanges. For this we must know the mutual needs of men; what each of us has to give and to get. Suppose there are ten men, each with ten kinds of needs, each applying himself to ten different kinds of work to provide for the necessities of life. The ten, because of differences of gift and talent, are likely to be less apt at some tasks than others, and all will be badly served when each does everything. But make a society of these ten, and let each man apply himself for his own benefit and that of the other nine to the kind of work that suits him best. Each one will profit by the talents of the others as if he personally had them all, and at the same time grow more perfect in his own line of work by constant practice. So it will come that the whole ten are perfectly provided for and will still have something left for others. This is the obvious basis of all our social institutions.

In this way the ideas of social relations take shape in the child's mind little by little, even before he becomes an active member of society himself. Emile sees that in order to have things for his own use he must have some he can exchange with other people. It is easy to lead him to feel the need for such exchanges and put himself in a position to profit by them.

As soon as he knows what life is, my first concern will be to teach him to preserve it. Up to this point I have ignored differences of station, rank or fortune, and I shall say little more about them in what follows, because man is the same in all stations. The rich man's stomach is no bigger than the poor man's, and his digestion no better. The master's arms are no longer and no stronger than the slave's. A 'great' man is no greater than a man of the people. Natural needs being everywhere alike, the means of satisfying them should likewise be equal. Fit man's education to what man really is. Do you not see that if you try to fit him exclusively for one way of life you make him useless for every other? You put your trust in the existing social order and do not take into account the fact that that order is subject to inevitable revolutions, and that you can neither foresee nor prevent the revolution that may affect your children. We are approaching a state of crisis and an age of revolution. It is impossible that the great monarchies of Europe should endure much longer. Who can tell what will happen then? What man has made, man can destroy. The only indestructible characters are those with nature's imprint, and nature makes neither princes, nor men of wealth, nor grand lords.

Of all the occupations in which a man can earn a living, manual work comes nearest the state of nature. The condition most independent of fortune and of man is that of the artisan. The artisan is a free man and depends only on his work: he is better off than the husbandman, bound to his fields, whose harvest may be taken from him by others. Nevertheless, agriculture is the first trade of man: the most worthy, the most useful, and consequently the most noble trade any one can practise. I do not say to Emile: 'study agriculture'. He is acquainted with it already. All the rural tasks are familiar to him. He began with them and he comes back to them regularly. What I say to him is: 'Cultivate the lands of your ancestors. But if you lose them, or have none to lose, learn a trade.'

So far as Emile is concerned the trade chosen is of no special consequence. A trade is only work with the hands, a mechanic art. His apprenticeship is more than half completed through the activities which have occupied him up to the present. What do you want him to do? He is ready for anything and everything. He can handle the spade and the hoe; he can use the turning lathe, the hammer, the plane or the file. He is already acquainted with the tools of all the trades. He only needs to acquire sufficient speed and ease in the use of any one of them to equal the competence of the good workmen whose they are; and he has one great advantage over them all in his agile body and his supple limbs. His organs are sound and well trained, and he knows the mechanical principles underlying the crafts. All he needs to enable him to work like a master is practical skill, and that comes with time.

All things considered, the trade I would like best for my pupil among those for which he has a taste would be that of a carpenter. It is clean; it is useful; it can be practised at home; it keeps the body in the fresh air; it requires dexterity and industry; and in the making of useful articles elegance and taste are not excluded. And if by chance the bent of your pupil is definitely towards the speculative sciences I should not object if you were to put him to a trade conformable with his inclinations. He might learn, for example, to make mathematical instruments, spectacles, telescopes and the like.

Unfortunately we cannot spend our whole time at the carpenter's bench. We are not only apprentice workmen; we are apprentice men, and the latter apprenticeship is harder and more lengthy than the other. My idea is that at least once or twice a week we should spend the whole day at our master's: getting up when he does, being at work before him, taking our meals with him, working under his orders; and after having had the honour of dining with his family we would go back to sleep on our own hard beds if we were so disposed. In this way we would learn several trades at once, and get a training in handicraft without neglecting the apprentice-ship to life.

Emile at the Age of Fifteen

Here is our child, ready to cease being a child and to enter on an individual life. More than ever he feels the necessity which binds him to things. After training his body and his senses, we have trained his mind and his judgment. In short, we have combined the use of his limbs with that of his faculties. We have made him an efficient thinking being and nothing further remains for us in the production of a complete man but to make him a loving, sensitive being: in fact, to perfect reason through sentiment. But before entering on this new order of things let us look back over the one we are leaving, and see where we have reached.

To begin with, our pupil had only sensations, now he has ideas: he had only feelings, now he judges; for from the comparison of several sensations, whether successive or simultaneous, and the judgment passed on them, there comes a sort of mixed or complex sensation which I call an idea. It is the particular way of forming ideas that gives its character to the human mind. A solid mind forms its ideas on real relations: a superficial one is content with appearances. Greater or less aptitude in the comparison of ideas and the discovery of relations is what makes the difference in the mental capacity of different people.

In sensation, judgment is purely passive—we feel what we feel: in perception or idea, it is active—it connects, compares, determines relations. It is never the sensation that is wrong but the judgment passed on it. The child says about the ice cream that it burns. That is a right sensation but a wrong judgment. So with the experiences of those who see a mirror for the first time, or enter a cellar at different times of the year, or dip a warm or cold hand into lukewarm water, or see the clouds passing over the moon as if they were stationary, or think the stick immersed in water is broken. All our mistakes in these cases come from judgment. Unfortunately social man is dependent on a great many things about which he has to judge. He must therefore be taught to reason correctly.

I will be told that in training the child to judge, I am departing from nature. I do not think so. Nature chooses her instruments, and makes use of them not according to opinion but according to necessity. There is a great difference between natural man living in nature and natural man living in the social state. Emile is not a savage to be banished to the deserts: he is a savage made to live in a town. He must know how to get a living in towns, and how to get on with their inhabitants, and to live with them, if not to live like them.

The best way of learning to judge correctly is to simplify our sense experiences as much as possible. To do this we must learn to check the reports of each sense by itself, over and above the check from the other senses. Then each sensation will become an idea, and this idea will always conform to the truth. This is the kind of acquirement I have tried to secure in this third stage of childhood.

Emile, who has been compelled to learn for himself and use his reason, has a limited knowledge, but the knowledge he has is his own, none of it half-known. Among the small number of things he really knows the most important is that there is much he does not know which he may one day come to know, much more that other people know that he will never know, and an infinity of things that nobody will ever know. He has a universal mind, not because of what he knows but from his faculty for acquiring knowledge: a mind open, intelligent, responsive, and (as Montaigne says) if not instructed, capable of being instructed. I am content if he knows the 'wherefore' of all he does, and the 'why' of all he believes.

The only knowledge Emile has at this stage is in the sphere of natural and physical facts. He does not even know the name of history, nor what metaphysics and ethics are. He knows the essential relations between man and things, but none of the moral relations between man and man. He has little ability to form general ideas or abstractions. He sees the qualities common to certain bodies without reasoning about the qualities in themselves. He knows abstract space by means of geometrical figures, and abstract quantity by means of algebraic symbols. These figures and signs are the basis of the abstractions, on which his senses rest. He does not seek to know things in themselves, but through the relations which interest him. He only judges external facts by their relation to himself, but this judgment of his is sound. Nothing fantastic or conventional enters into it. He sets most store on what is useful for him, and as he never departs from this method of evaluation, he is not swayed by accepted opinion.

Emile is hard working, temperate, patient, stable and courageous. His imagination, still unstimulated, does not exaggerate dangers. Few evils affect him and he can endure suffering calmly because he has learned not to fight against fate. As for death, he does not yet know what it is, but being accustomed to submit unresistingly to the laws of nature, he will die if he must without a struggle. To live a free man and hold human affairs lightly is the best way to prepare for death. In a word, Emile has every personal virtue. To add the social virtues he only needs to know the relations which call them into being. That knowledge his mind is now quite ready to receive.

He still thinks of himself without regard to others and is quite satisfied that others should give no thought to him. He asks nothing from other people and does not believe that he owes anything to them. Thus far he stands alone in human society. He is self-dependent and is better entitled to be so than any other person, since he is all that a child could be at his age. He has no mistaken ideas and no vices, other than those that nobody can avoid. He has a healthy body, agile limbs, a true mind free from prejudice, a free heart devoid of passion. Self-esteem, the first and most natural of all the passions, has still to awaken in him. Without disturbing anybody's peace he has lived happy, contented and free within the bounds of nature. Do you think that a child who has reached his fifteenth year like this has wasted his childhood?

BOOK FOUR

ADOLESCENCE

Editorial Note

Adolescence is the time of the New Birth when the boy passes into his manhood. Awakening sex transforms both body and mind. Up to this time he has been absorbed in himself and the physical world around him. Now with new passions and new understanding, he enters the moral sphere. Self-love, hitherto self-centred, takes social form as self-esteem and brings him into personal relations with his fellows. The main urge is for a sex mate, an urge which gradually becomes more and more conscious till by the end of the period it becomes the chief inspiring and restraining influence in his life. As before, Rousseau is insistent on the need for retarding development so that the healthy natural inclinations of the young adolescent may not be overwhelmed by the prejudices of an artificial society. With this in view, he plans for Emile a gradual entry into community life: beginning with the personal relationships of friendship and human helpfulness (at 16); going on to the wider acquaintance with mankind that comes through history and religion, with the youth as spectator rather than participant (at 18); ending with his introduction to the polite society of a great city and the cultivation of good taste through literature and drama (at 20).

The educational scheme propounded for this stage does not differ greatly from that generally followed in the case of young men of rank everywhere in eighteenth century Europe. The main studies recommended were those pursued by most cultured people of the period, with literature and languages as the core, and Emile goes on the grand tour to learn the ways of the world and acquire the tastes of a gentleman.

There is perhaps more stress laid on the social studies, bt the sciences begun in the pre-adolescent years have no place; and the motive for learning is not found in the need for preparing for a career, but in preparation for an ideal marriage. Apart from the fact that the tutor is specially concerned to keep his young charge within the bounds of a puritanical code of conduct, he does not differ greatly from the scholarly companions of other young men of the time.

EMILE AT SIXTEEN: THE AGE OF FRIENDSHIP

The Beginnings of Adolescence

We are born twice over; the first time for existence, the second for life; once as human beings and later as men or as women. Up to puberty, children of the two sexes have nothing obvious to distinguish them. They are similar in features, in figure, in complexion, in voice. Girls are children, boys are children. The same name suffices for beings so much alike.

But man is not meant to remain a child for ever. At the time prescribed by nature he passes out of his childhood. As the fretting of the sea precedes the distant storm, this disturbing change is announced by the murmur of nascent passions. A change of mood, frequent tantrums, a constant unease of mind make the child hard to manage. He no longer listens to his master's voice. He is a lion in a fever. He mistrusts his guide and is averse to control.

With the moral signs of changing mood go patent physical changes. His countenance develops and takes on the imprint of a definite character. The soft slight down on his cheeks grows darker and firmer. His voice breaks, or rather, gets lost. He is neither child nor man, and he speaks like neither. His eyes, organs of the soul, which have hitherto said nothing, find language and expression as they light up with a new fire. He is becoming conscious that they can tell too much and he is learning to lower them and blush. He is disturbed for no reason whatever.

This is the second birth of which I spoke. Now is the time that man really enters into life and finds nothing alien to him. So far his guardian's responsibility has been child's play: it is only now that his task comes to have real importance. This stage at which ordinary educations end is just that when ours should begin.

The passions are the chief instruments for our preservation. The child's first sentiment is self-love, the only passion that is born with man. The second, which is derived from it, is the love he has for the people he sees ready to help him, and from this develops a kindly feeling for mankind. But with fresh needs and growing dependence on others comes the consciousness of social relations and with it the sense of duties and preferences. It is at this point that the child may become domineering, jealous, deceitful, vindictive. Self-love being concerned only with ourselves is content when our real needs are satisfied, but self-esteem which involves comparisons with other people never is and never can be content because it makes the impossible demand that others should prefer us to themselves. That is how it comes that the gentle kindly passions issue from self-love, while hate and anger spring from self-esteem. Great care and skill are required to prevent the human heart being depraved by the new needs of social life.

The proper study of man is that of his relationships. So long as he is aware of himself only as a physical being he should study himself in his relations with things. That is the task of childhood. When he comes to consciousness of himself as a moral being he should study himself in his relations with his fellows. This is the occupation of his whole life, beginning at the point we have now reached.

The Development of the Passions

As soon as a man has need of a mate he ceases to be a solitary creature. Forthwith all his relations with humanity and all the affections of his soul come into being. His first passion makes all the rest active.

The time of transition from childhood to adolescence is not absolutely fixed by nature but varies in individuals with temperament, and in races with climatic conditions. Everybody knows the differences in this respect between hot and cold countries, and is aware that ardent temperaments mature earlier than others. But it is possible to be mistaken about the causes and to attribute to physical factors what is due to moral. This is one of the commonest blunders of the philosophy of our times. Nature's instructions are slow and leisurely: those of man are almost always premature. In the first case, the senses arouse the imagination; in the second the imagination arouses the senses and gives them a precocious activity. It is a fact to be noted that puberty and sexual potency always come earlier among educated and civilised peoples than among those that are ignorant and barbarous. Children are singularly quick to see through the sham decency that covers bad morals. The refined language they must use, the lessons they get in propriety, the veil of mystery put over their eyes only serve to stimulate their curiosity. It is plain from the way in which it is done that they are expected to learn what is concealed. Of all the instruction they get, none profits them more.

If you consult experience, you will understand how much this very foolish method does to hurry on the work of nature and to ruin the character. This is one of the chief causes of racial degeneration in towns. Young people, drained of their energy at an early age remain small, weakly, badly built, and grow old before their time, like the vine that has been forced to bear fruit in the spring, which droops and dies before autumn.

It is evident that if the variation in the age at which man becomes conscious of sex is due as much to education as to the action of nature, this time of life may be hastened or retarded by the kind of education children get. And if the body gains or loses in stability by retardation or acceleration, it is also evident that the longer we are able to retard it, the greater will be the vigour and strength a young man acquires.

From these considerations I derive the solution of the much debated question whether it is better to enlighten children early on the matters of their curiosity, or to deceive them with modest misstatements. I do not think it is necessary to take either the one course or the other. In the first place, this curiosity only comes if the opportunity offers, and that we must prevent. In the second place, questions that we are not compelled to settle do not call for a deceitful answer. It is better to tell the questioner to be quiet than to answer with a lie. But if an answer has to be given, it should be given with perfect simplicity, with no mystery or embarrassment and not even a smile. There is much less danger in satisfying a child's curiosity than in exciting it. I need not add that the answer should be true. It is impossible to warn children against lying to their elders unless these elders realise how much worse it is to lie to children. A single lie the pupil has found his teacher telling him will ruin for ever the fruit of education.

Absolute ignorance on certain matters is perhaps best for children. But they should be taught quite early anything that cannot be hidden from them. Either their curiosity should not be roused in any way whatever, or it should be satisfied before the age at which it may possibly do harm. If your pupil cannot be kept ignorant of sex differences up to sixteen make sure he learns about them before ten.

The only satisfactory way of preserving children's innocence is to have about them people who respect it. Without this all the care we take to keep them ignorant will sooner or later fail. A smile, a twinkle of the eye, a passing gesture will show them that something is being hidden from them. When we truly respect their simplicity it is easy to find fitting words in talking to them. There is a certain artless manner of speech which diverts them from a dangerous curiosity.

'Where do babies come from?', an embarrassing question which comes quite naturally to children. The answer to it whether wise or foolish may affect a child's morals and health all his life. The shortest way for a mother to escape from it without deceiving her son is to tell him to be quiet. That would be all right if he was perfectly used to getting that answer in matters of indifference, and there was no suspicion of mystery in a new tone of voice. Will you allow me to tell you a reply I once heard given to the question, which impressed me all the more because it came from a woman of modest speech and manners, who was able at need to disregard the false fear of blame and the idle talk of foolish people, for the sake of her son's welfare. 'Mamma,' said the little scatterbrain, 'where do babies come from?' 'Sonny,' the mother replied without hesitation, 'women pass them with pains that sometimes cost them their lives.' Let fools laugh or be shocked, but wise people will seek in vain for a more judicious reply or one better fit to serve its purpose.

If you want to regulate the nascent passions, extend

the period of their development so that they may have time to adjust themselves as they arise. Then it will not be man who controls them but nature herself. All you have to do is to leave it to her to manage her own work. If your pupil were alone there would be nothing for you to do at all. But everything around him inflames his imagination. The torrent of prejudices carries him along; to hold him back you must push in the opposite direction. Sentiment must restrain imagination, and reason silence the opinions of men. The source of all the passions is the sensibility, but imagination determines the course they take. It is the errors of imagination that convert the passions into vices.

The First Social Sentiments

So long as a child's feelings are confined to himself, his actions have no moral character. It is only when they begin to take him beyond himself that he first forms the sentiments, and later the ideas of good and evil which make him truly man and an integral part of humanity. It is on this point that we must fix attention in the first place. To do so we must reject the example of those sophisticated children who are men in thought long before they are really men, and look for those in whom the successive developments follow the course of nature.

The onward movement of nature is slow and unhurried. Gradually the blood grows warm, the vital spirits develop, the character gets formed. The wise workman who directs the task takes care to perfect all the instruments before putting then to work. A long-continued unease precedes the first desires, a deep ignorance masks their significance. The youth desires he knows not what. The blood ferments. The eye brightens and surveys other beings. There is a

new interest in all the people around, a new feeling that
one was not meant to live alone. It is in this way that the
heart opens to the human affections and becomes capable
of attachment.

The first sentiment to which a well brought up young
man is susceptible is not love but friendship. The first
act of his awakening imagination is to show him that
there are people like himself: mankind comes before sex.
Here is another advantage of a prolonged innocence.
You can take advantage of the new sensibility to implant
the first seeds of humanity in the heart of the young
adolescent. A young man brought up in happy simplicity
is drawn by the first movements of nature to the tender
kindly passions. His compassionate heart is affected by
the sufferings of his fellows. He thrills with delight when
he meets a comrade. If the warmth of his blood makes
him quick to anger you see the goodness of his heart a
minute later in his effusive repentance. Yes, I maintain
without fear of contradiction that a well-born boy who
has preserved his innocence to the age of twenty is the
most generous and most lovable of men.

It is the weakness of men that makes them social beings.
Our common sufferings incline our hearts to humanity.
Every attachment is a token of insufficiency. If it were
not that everyone of us had need of other people, we would
scarcely think of associating with them. From our very
infirmity comes our frail happiness.

If you want to encourage in a young man's heart the
first promptings of a nascent sensibility and make him
kindly and good, do not let pride, vanity and envy grow
up in him by giving him a misleading vision of human
happiness. Do not let him view the pomp of courts
and the attractions of pageantry, or take him into
high society. To show him the world before he knows

mankind is not to make a man of him but to corrupt him; is not to instruct him but to lead him astray. All men are born poor and naked, subject to ills and sufferings of every kind, condemned in the end to die. This is what man's lot really is, and with this the study of human nature should begin.

At sixteen the adolescent knows about suffering because he himself has suffered, but he barely knows that other beings also suffer; seeing without feeling is not knowledge. But when the first development of the senses kindles in him the fire of imagination, he begins to feel himself in his fellows and to share in their sufferings. It is at this point that the sad picture of humanity should bring to his heart the first compassion he has ever experienced. So is born pity, the first social sentiment that affects the human heart according to the order of nature.

All this may be summed up in three maxims. First: it is not in human nature to put ourselves in the place of people happier than ourselves, only in the place of those who are more to be pitied. Second: we only pity the misfortunes of others when we believe that we are not exempt from them ourselves (*Non ignara mali, miseris succurrere disco*: *Aeneid* I, 630). Third: the pity we feel for the ills of others does not depend on the amount of these ills but on the feeling we attribute to the sufferers.

In effect, my method is this. On the approach of the critical age, show young people sights which restrain rather than excite them. Give direction to the imagination by means of objects which minimise its activity. Keep them away from large towns where the dress and immodest behaviour of the women speeds up the lessons of nature, and where they get a sight of pleasures which they would be better not to know till they can make their own choices. Take them back to the homes of their childhood where the simple life of the country allows the passions of their age to develop less rapidly. Or if their taste for the arts keeps them in town, save them from a dangerous idleness by this very taste. Make careful choice of their company, their occupations and their pleasures. Keep in mind also that there is danger of excess everywhere, and that immoderate passions always work lasting harm. I am not suggesting that you should make your pupil a sick-nurse or a brother of charity, to afflict his sight with continual views of pain and suffering as he goes from one hospital to another, or from the gallows to the prison. You want him to be touched but not hardened by the sight of human miseries. Your pupil should know something about the lot of man and the troubles of his fellows, but should not witness them too often. A single object well chosen and seen at a suitable time will produce a feeling of pity, and give him something to think about for a month. By a sparing use of examples, lessons and pictures, you may quieten the urge of the senses and sidetrack nature, even when you are following her own directions.

Teachers complain that the impetuosity of this age makes youth insubordinate, and I see it myself. But is it not their own fault? Do they not realise that once they have allowed this ardour to find expression through the senses, no other way is possible? So far from this adolescent fire being an obstacle to education, it is by means of it that education is brought to completion. It gives the guardian a hold on the heart of the young man when he ceases to be the stronger. The youth's first affections are the reins by which all his movements can be directed once he is free. So long as he loved nothing he depended only on himself. As soon as he loves, he depends on those to whom he is attached. In this way are forged the first links that bind him to mankind. But do not imagine that his new born affections will embrace all men. To begin with, this attachment will be confined to his fellows, and his fellows will only be those with whom he associates, people who think and feel like himself and have similar pains and pleasures, those in short whose obvious identity of nature with himself increases his self-love. It will only be after he has developed his native dispositions in a thousand ways and reflected long on the sentiments he observes in himself and others, that he will succeed in comprehending his individual notions under the abstract idea of humanity and combining his personal affections with those that identify him with mankind.

EMILE AT EIGHTEEN: THE AGE OF HUMANITY

Social Education

At last we are entering the moral sphere. We have reached the second stage of manhood. If this were the place for it, I would try to show how the first impulses of the heart give rise to the first utterances of conscience, and how from the sentiments of love and hate come the first ideas of good and evil. I would demonstrate that justice and goodness are not merely abstract terms, moral entities created by the understanding, but real affections of the soul enlightened by reason which have developed from our primitive affections. I would show too that it is impossible to establish any natural law by reason alone, independent of conscience, and that natural rights are an empty dream unless they are based on the natural needs of the human heart. But I do not think I am called on to write treatises on metaphysics and ethics or detail any courses of study whatever.

Up to the present, my Emile has thought only about

himself. The first thought he gives to his fellows leads him to compare himself with them; and the first sentiment excited in him by this comparison is a desire for priority. It is at this point that self-love changes into self-esteem and that all the passions pertaining to the latter begin to be active. But to determine whether the passions which will dominate his character are to be humane and kindly, or cruel and malevolent, we must know what he regards as his proper place among men and what kind of obstacles he thinks he will have to overcome to reach it. We have already let him see the chances of life which are common to all mankind. We must now for his guidance in this quest show him the differences among men and give him a picture of the whole social order.

Here it is important to take the opposite course from the one we have been following so far, and let the young man learn from other people's experience rather than his own. I would have you choose a young man's associates so that he may think well of those who live with him, and at the same time I would have you teach him to know the world so well that he may think ill of all that goes on in it. You want him to know and feel that man is naturally good, and to judge his neighbour by himself: equally, you want him to see how society corrupts men and to find in their prejudices the source of all their vices. This method, I have to admit, has its drawbacks and it is not easy to put into practice. If a young man is set to observe men too early and too close up, he will take a hateful pleasure in interpreting everything as badness and fail to see anything good in what is really good. Soon the general perversity will serve him as an excuse rather than as a warning, and he will say that if this is what man is, he himself has no wish to be different.

To get over this obstacle and bring him to an understanding of the human heart without risk of spoiling himself I would show him men in other times and places, in such a way that he can look on the scene as an outsider. This is the time for history. By means of it he will read the hearts of men without the lessons of philosophy, and look on them as a mere spectator without prejudice and without passion: judging them, but neither their accomplice nor their accuser.

Unfortunately this study has dangers and drawbacks of various kinds. It is difficult to put one's self at a point of view from which to judge one's fellows fairly. One of the great vices of history is the portrayal of men by what is bad in them rather than by what is good. It is from revolutions and catastrophes that it derives its interest. So long as a nation grows and prospers in the calm of peaceful government, history has nothing to say about it. It only begins to tell about nations when they are no longer self-sufficient and have got mixed up in their neighbours' affairs. It only records their story when they enter on their decline. Our historians all begin where they ought to finish. Only bad men achieve fame: the good are either forgotten or held up to ridicule. Like philosophy, history always slanders mankind.

Moreover, the facts described in history never give an exact picture of what actually happened. They change form in the historian's head. They get moulded by his interests and take on the hue of his prejudices. Who can put the reader at the precise point where an event can be seen just as it took place? Ignorance or partisanship distorts everything. Without even altering a single feature a quite different face can be put on events by a broader or a narrower view of the relevant circumstances. How often a tree more or less, a rock to the right or the left, a cloud of dust blown up by the wind, have decided the outcome of a battle without anybody being aware of it! But that does not prevent the historian telling you the causes of defeat or victory with as much assurance as if he had been everywhere himself. In any case, what do the facts matter when the reason for them is unknown? And what lessons can I draw from an event when I am ignorant of the real cause of it? The historian gives me an explanation, but it is his own invention. And is not criticism itself, of which there is so much talk, only an art of guessing, the art of choosing among various lies the one most like the truth?

I will be told that historical precision is of less consequence than the truth about men and manners. So long as the human heart is well depicted, it will be said, it does not greatly matter whether events are accurately narrated or not. That is right, if the pictures are drawn close enough to nature. If, however, most of them are coloured by the historian's imagination, we are back again to the difficulty we set out to avoid, and are allowing writers an authority which has been denied the teacher. If my pupil is only to see pictures of fancy, I prefer to have them traced by my own hand. They will at least be those best suited for him.*

The worst historians for a young man are those who pass judgment. Give him the facts and let him judge for himself. That is how he will learn to know men. If he is always guided by some author's judgment, he only sees through another's eyes: when he lacks these eyes he cannot see.

I put modern history aside, not only because there is a lack of distinctive character about men nowadays, but

* Book II. ' Men of sense should regard history as a tissue of fables, the moral of which is peculiarly appropriate to the human heart.'

because our historians are so much concerned with producing an impression that they aim mainly at making highly coloured portraits, often representing nothing much. The ancients as a rule go in less for portraiture, and put more of intuition and less of conscious thought into their judgment. In my opinion Thucydides is the model historian. He relates the facts without passing judgment on them, and yet he omits none of the essential circumstances which we must know in forming our judgment. He puts the whole story under the reader's eyes. So far from coming between the events and the reader he keeps himself out of sight. You get the sense of seeing rather than of reading. Unfortunately he speaks of nothing but war, and most of his stories are about battles, the least edifying thing in the world. *The Retreat of the Ten Thousand* and Caesar's *Commentaries* have almost the same wisdom and the same weakness. The good Herodotus, fluent, artless and full of most pleasing detail, would perhaps be the best of historians if his details did not often degenerate into a childish simplicity which is more likely to spoil the taste of youth than to form it. He has to be read with discretion. I say nothing about Livy: his turn will come, but he is a politician and a rhetorician, and is altogether unsuited for pupils of this age.

The defect of most history is that it only keeps record of the obvious outstanding facts which can be fixed by names, places and dates. But the slow-moving, cumulative causes of the facts which cannot be fixed in this way remain unknown. We often find in a battle lost or won the reason for a revolution which even before had become inevitable. War only makes evident events already determined by moral causes, which historians are rarely able to appreciate.

To all these considerations must be added the fact

that history is more concerned with actions than with men. It takes men at certain chosen moments when they are in full dress. It only depicts the public man when he is prepared to be seen, and does not follow him into the intimacies of friendship and private life. It is the coat rather than the person that is portrayed.

I would much rather have the study of human nature begin with the reading of the life story of individual men. In these stories the historian gets on the track of the man, and there is no escape from his scrutiny. 'The writers most to my mind,' says Montaigne, 'are biographers, because they find ideas more entertaining than events, and delight more in what comes from within than from without. That is why Plutarch is the man for me in every way.'

It is true that the genius of nations, or of men in association, is very different from the character of man as an individual; and the knowledge of human nature got without examination of the form it assumes in the multitude, would be very imperfect. But it is no less true that it is necessary to begin with the study of man in order to form a judgment about men, and that one who had a complete knowledge of the dispositions of the constituent individuals might be able to foresee their joint effects in the body politic.

Plutarch excels in the use he makes of detail. He has an inimitable grace in depicting great men in the little things, and is so happy in the choice of their traits that often a word or a smile or a gesture suffices to characterise his hero. With a joke Hannibal reassures his frightened army, and leads them laughing into battle. Agesilaus riding on a pole makes me love the conqueror of the great king. Alexander swallows a draught without saying a word—it is the finest moment in his life. This is the real art of portraiture. The essential features are not shown in the great traits, nor the character in great deeds. It is in the trifles that a man's nature is revealed.

The Cure for Vanity

One step more and we reach the goal. Self-esteem is a useful instrument but it has its dangers. Often it wounds the hand that employs it and rarely does good without also doing evil. Emile, comparing himself with other human beings and finding himself very fortunately situated, will be tempted to give credit to his own reason for the work of his guardian, and to attribute to his own merit the effects of his good fortune. He will say: 'I am wise, and men are foolish'. This is the error most to be feared, because it is the one hardest to eradicate. If choice had to be made I do not know whether I would not prefer the illusion of prejudice to the illusion of pride.

There is no remedy for vanity but experience. It is doubtful indeed if it can be cured at all; but at any rate its growth may be checked when it appears. Do not waste your time on fine arguments and try to convince an adolescent that he is a man like other men and subject to the same weaknesses. Make him feel it for himself, or he will never learn it. Once again, I have to make an exception to my own rules, by deliberately exposing my pupil to the mischances which may prove to him that he is no wiser than the rest of us. I will let flatterers get the better of him. If fools were to entice him into some extravagance or other I would let him run the risk. I will allow him to be duped by card sharpers, and leave him to be swindled by them. The only snares from which I would guard him with special care would be those of prostitutes. Actually Emile would not be readily tempted in these ways. It should be kept in mind that my constant plan is to take things at their worst. I try in the first place to prevent the vice, and then I assume its existence in order to show how it can be remedied.

The time for faults is the time for fables. Censure of an offender under cover of a fiction gives instruction without offence. The young man learns in this way that the moral of the tale is not a lie, from the truth that finds application in his own case. The child who has never been deceived by flattery sees no point in the fable of *The Fox and the Crow*, but the silly person who has been gulled by a flatterer understands perfectly what a fool the crow was. From a fact he draws a moral, and the experience which would speedily have been forgotten is engraved in his mind by the fable. There is no moral knowledge which cannot be acquired either through the experience of other people or of ourselves. Where the experience is too dangerous for the young man to get it at first hand, the lesson can be drawn from history. When the test has no serious consequences it is good for him to be exposed to it and to have the particular cases known to him summed up as maxims. I do not mean, however, that these maxims should be expounded or even stated. The moral at the end of most fables is badly conceived. Before I put the inimitable fables of La Fontaine into the hands of a young man I would cut out all the conclusions in which he takes the trouble to explain what he had just said so clearly and agreeably. If your pupil does not understand the fable without the explanation, you can be sure that he will not understand it in any case. Only men can learn from fables and now is the time for Emile to begin.

When I see young people confined to the speculative studies at the most active time of life and then cast suddenly into the world of affairs without the least experience, I find it as contrary to reason as to nature and am not at all surprised that so few people manage their lives well. By some strange perversity we are taught all sorts of useless things, but nothing is done about the art of conduct. We are supposed to be getting trained for society but are taught as if each one of us were going to live a life of contemplation in a solitary cell. You think you are preparing children for life when you teach them certain bodily contortions and meaningless strings of words. I also have been a teacher of the art of conduct. I have taught my Emile to live his own life, and more than that to earn his own bread. But that is not enough. To live in the world one must get on with people and know how to get a hold on them. It is necessary also to be able to estimate the action and reaction of individual interests in civil society and so forecast events as to be rarely at fault in one's enterprises.

It is by doing good that we become good. I know of no surer way. Keep your pupil occupied with all the good deeds within his power. Let him help poor people with money and with service, and get justice for the oppressed. Active benevolence will lead him to reconcile the quarrels of his comrades and to be concerned about the sufferings of the afflicted. By putting his kindly feelings into action in this way and drawing his own conclusions from the outcome of his efforts, he will get a great deal of useful knowledge. In addition to college lore he will acquire the still more important ability of applying his knowledge to the purposes of life.

Religious Education

My readers, I foresee, will be surprised to see me take my pupil through the whole of the early years without mentioning religion. At fifteen he was not aware that he had a soul, and perhaps at eighteen it is not yet time for him to learn. For if he learns sooner than is necessary he runs the risk of never knowing.

My picture of hopeless stupidity is a pedant teaching the catechism to children. If I wanted to make a child dull I would compel him to explain what he says when he repeats his catechism. It may be objected that since most of the Christian doctrines are mysteries it would be necessary for the proper understanding of them to wait, not merely till the child becomes a man but till the man is no more. To that I reply, in the first place, that there are mysteries man can neither conceive nor believe and that I see no purpose in teaching them to children unless it be to teach them to lie. I say, further, that to admit there are mysteries one must understand that they are incomprehensible, and that this is an idea which is quite beyond children. For an age when all is mystery, there can be no mysteries, properly so-called.

Let us be on guard against presenting the truth to those unable to comprehend it. The effect of that is to substitute error for truth. It would be better to have no idea of the Divine Being than to have ideas that are mean, fantastic and unworthy. 'I would rather people believed there was no Plutarch in the world,' says the good Plutarch, 'than that it should be said that he was unjust, envious, jealous, and such a tyrant that he exacts more than can be performed.'

The worst thing about the distorted images of the Deity imprinted on children's minds, is that they endure all their lives, so that even when they grow up their God is still the God of their childhood. Every child who believes in God is an idolater, or rather he thinks of God in human shape. Once the imagination has seen

God, it is very seldom that the understanding conceives Him. I once met in Switzerland a good pious mother who was so convinced of this that she would not teach her son religion in his early years, for fear he might be content with this crude instruction and neglect a better when he came to the age of reason. This child never heard God spoken about save with devotion and reverence, and he was silenced when he tried to speak of Him, on the ground that the subject was too great and too sublime for him. This reserve roused his curiosity, and his pride made him look forward to the time when he would know the mystery so carefully hidden from him. The less that was said about God the more he thought of Him. The child saw God everywhere. My own fear is that this air of mystery might excite a young man's imagination overmuch and turn his head so that he would become a fanatic rather than a believer.

But there is no fear of anything like that happening with my Emile. He always refuses to pay any attention to everything beyond his grasp and hears with indifference things he does not understand. When he does begin to be troubled by these great questions, it will not be because they have been put before him, but because the natural progress of his intelligence is taking his inquiries in that direction.

At this point I see a difficulty ahead: a difficulty all the greater because it is due less to the facts of the situation than to the cowardice of those who are afraid to face up to it. Let us at least be bold enough to state the problem. A child has to be brought up in his father's religion, and always gets ample proof that this religion, whatever it is, is the only true one, and all the others are absurd and ridiculous. In matters of religion more than in any other opinion triumphs. What then are we, who profess to cast

off the yoke of opinion and seek to be independent of
authority, to do about this? We do not wish to teach our
Emile anything which he could not learn for himself
in any country. In what religion are we to bring him up?
With which sect is the man of nature to be connected?
The answer it seems to me is very simple. We will not
make him join this sect or that, but put him in the position
to choose the one to which he himself is led by the best
use of his reason.

NOTE: At this point Rousseau breaks off from the story
of Emile to give an exposition of natural religion in a
tractate entitled *The Confession of Faith of the Savoyard
Curate* which occupies an eighth part of the whole book.
The spokesman is a lovable Catholic priest who be-
friended Rosseau and gave him spiritual guidance in the
days of his vagabondage, but the *Confession* is Rousseau's
own. The opening section is a discussion of the fundamen-
tals of belief in which Rousseau, following the illustrious
Clarke [Dr. Samuel Clarke (1675-1729), an English divine,
author of a *Discourse concerning the Being and Attributes
of God*], refutes the materialistic doctrines of contem-
porary philosophers. From this he proceeds to the discussion of religious dogmas depending on revelation,
and concludes by finding the Inner Light sufficient to
give all the direction in religion that man needs in
matters of practical consequence.

So long as we take no account of the authority of man
or the prejudices of the country of our birth and educate
according to nature, the light of reason by itself can lead
us no further than to natural religion: and to that I
confine myself with Emile. If he is to have another
religion I have no longer the right to be his guide. The
choice is his alone.

We are working in concert with nature. While she is

forming the physical man we are seeking to form the moral man; but the two do not progress at the same rate. The body is already strong and sturdy while the soul remains dull and feeble, and in spite of all that human skill can do the temperament is always ahead of the reason. So far as we have gone our main endeavour has been to hold back the one side and bring on the other so that as far as possible the man we are training may be at one with himself. In developing his nature we have controlled his sensibility by cultivating the reason. By taking him to the essence of things we have saved him from the domination of the senses. It has been easy to lead him from the study of nature to the search for its Author.

In doing this we have gained a fresh hold on our pupil. It is only now that he has come to have a real interest in being good and doing good, whether anyone sees him or not and without the compulsion of law; and is concerned to be on right terms with God and do his duty whatever the cost. He has learned to cherish virtue not merely for the love of social order (which for all of us is subordinate to the love of self) but for the love of the Author of his being which enters into his self-love, so that in the end he may enjoy the lasting happiness which peace of conscience and the contemplation of God promise him in another life after he has made good use of the present life.

EMILE AT TWENTY: THE AGE OF LOVE

The Coming of Manhood

Nature's hour has come at last, as come it must. Since man must die he must reproduce in order to carry on the species and keep the world going. As soon as you

have a presentiment of the critical time give up once
and for all your former manner of speech. The boy is
still your disciple but he is no longer your pupil. He is
your friend but a man. Henceforth treat him as such.

What course are we to take? It is commonly thought
that the alternative is to indulge his desires, or to combat
them. The consequences in either case are so serious that
one may well hesitate in choosing between them.

The first way of escape from the difficulty that suggests
itself is an early marriage. But though this is the surest
and most natural plan, I doubt whether as things are it
is the best or the most satisfactory. I agree that it would
be a good thing if young people could marry at the
nubile age. But this age comes for them before its proper
time. Marriage should be postponed till maturity.

Seeing that there is no fixed term for natural development, I think I may assume that, thanks to my care,
Emile remains in his first innocence up to this time, but
I see that this happy period is near its end. He is sur-
rounded by ever increasing temptations and whatever I
do he is going to get away from me before very long.
There is now only one reasonable course to take. I must
make him responsible for his own actions, safeguard him
against unexpected blunders, and show him plainly the
perils that beset him. Hitherto I have controlled him by
his ignorance: now the control must come from
knowledge.

Keep in mind that in directing an adult you must
follow the opposite method from that used with a child.
Do not hesitate to instruct him in those dangerous
mysteries which you have hidden from him so long and
so carefully. Since he must come to know them it is
important that he should learn them from you and not
from somebody else, or by himself.

Some of my readers while adopting my ideas may think that all that is called for is an incidental conversation with the young man. But that assuredly is not the way to manage the human heart. What is said will be of no effect unless there has been due preparation. Before sowing, the ground must be tilled. The seeds of virtue are slow to grow, and there must be a lengthy period of cultivation before they take root. Judge whether the time when the inflamed senses are distracting the understanding and dominating the will is the right time for listening to the grave lessons of wisdom. Therefore, never talk reason with young men even at the age of reason, unless you have first made them ready to hear.

Reading, solitude, idleness, a soft sedentary life, the company of women and young people are a constant danger for young men. I divert Emile's senses by other objects of sense. I turn his mind in a different direction from the one it is beginning to take. I halt the misleading activity of imagination by strenuous physical exercises. When the limbs are busy, imagination is quiet. When the body is tired, the heart does not become heated. The quickest and easiest precaution is to take him out of the immediate danger, but that is not enough. I began by taking him away from towns and their temptations. But there is no desert place to which he can go to escape from his own imaginings. Unless I can take him away from dangerous objects and memories, and distract him from himself, I might as well leave him where he is.

Emile has a trade, but this trade does not meet the need. He loves and understands agriculture, but agriculture is not enough. The occupations he knows become a routine and do not occupy his mind. He can think of something quite different while at work: head and arms act independently. What he requires is a new occupation that will interest by its novelty and absorb his thoughts completely. The only one that seems to me to satisfy all the conditions is hunting. If hunting is ever an innocent pleasure worthy of a man, now is the time for it. I do not mean that the whole of Emile's youth should be spent in the slaughter of animals, and I do not even pretend to justify this cruel passion. It is enough for me that it serves to hold back a more dangerous passion and allows him to listen to me calmly when I speak about it.

The Ideal Woman

Emile is not destined to remain a solitary for ever. He is a member of society and must fulfil its obligations. Destined to live with men, he has to know them. He knows man in general already; the next thing is for him to know individual men. He knows what goes on in the world: the next thing is for him to know how people live in it. The time has come to take him to the front of that great stage, of which he already knows the hidden workings. He will not look on it now with the foolish wonder of a young dolt, but with the discrimination of a sober, straightforward, thinking man.

As there is a fitting time for the study of the sciences, so is there a time for getting a good understanding of the ways of the world. Anyone who learns these ways too young follows them without proper discrimination or reflection his whole life long. But one who learns them with an appreciation of the reasons for them, follows them with greater discernment and in consequence more exactly and more finely. Give me a child of twelve who knows nothing at all, and at fifteen I will give him back to you as wise as the one you have instructed from the beginning. The difference will be that your child will have his knowledge in his memory, while mine will have it in his judgment. Similarly a young man of twenty introduced into the world under proper guidance will become more agreeable and more refined in a year's time than one who has been brought up in it from the beginning.

You need a mate, I say to the young man. Let us go in search of one to suit you. We may not find her easily, since real merit is always rare. But we will not hurry, and we will not be discouraged. Without doubt there is such a person and in the end we will find her, or some one very like her. With this attractive project I introduce him into society. What need to say more?

You can see that in portraying the destined mistress I will be able to make dear and pleasing to him the qualities he ought to love, and set his mind against the things he should avoid. I would have to be very stupid if I did not rouse his passions in anticipation of the unknown woman. The fact that the picture I paint is an imaginary one is of no consequence. People are more in love with the image they make for themselves than with its object. To see what we love exactly as it is, would make an end of love on the earth.

For all that, I do not mean that we should deceive a young man by painting a model of perfection who could never exist. But I will choose his mistress's defects so that they will suit him and give him pleasure and serve to correct his own. If he is satisfied with the picture it will not be long before he desires an original for it. I would go so far as to put a name to her. I would say with a smile: 'Let us call your mistress, Sophie. Sophie is a name of good omen. If the girl you choose does not bear it, she will at any rate be worthy of the name.' If the features to be put before him have been well chosen the rest will be easy. There will then be little risk in letting him go appearance will be simple and unpretentious. He neither has nor desires the qualities that make an immediate impression. He sets too little store by the opinions of men to be concerned about their prejudices, and is not concerned to have people esteem him till they know him. His way of presenting himself is neither modest nor conceited, but just natural and sincere. He knows neither constraint nor concealment. He is the same in company as when he is alone. He speaks little, because he has no desire to attract notice. For the same reason he only speaks about things that are of practical value, being too well informed ever to be a babbler. Far from despising the ways of other people, he conforms quite readily to them: not for the sake of appearing versed in the conventions or affecting fashionable airs, but simply to avoid notice. He is never more at his ease than when nobody is paying him any attention.

When he studies the ways of men in society as he formerly studied their passions in history, he will often have occasion to reflect on the things that gratify or offend the human heart. This will lead him to philosophise on the principles of taste, and this is the study that is most fitting for this period of life.

There is no need to go far for a definition of taste. Taste is simply the faculty of judging what pleases or displeases the greatest number of people. This does not mean that there are more people of taste than others. For though the majority judge sanely about any particular thing, there are few who possess this sanity about everything. Taste is like beauty. Though the most general tastes put together make good taste, there are not many people of taste, just as beauty is constituted by an assemblage of the most common traits and yet there are few beautiful persons.

We are not concerned here with the things we like because they are useful, or dislike because they are harmful. Taste has nothing to do with the necessities of life: it applies to things which are indifferent to us or at most have the interest that goes with our amusements. This is what makes decisions of taste so difficult and seemingly so arbitrary. I should add that taste has local rules which make it dependent in very many ways on region, custom, government and institutions, as well as other rules relating to age, sex and character. That is why there can be no disputing about tastes.

Taste is natural to all men, but all do not possess it in equal measure. The degree of taste we may have depends on native sensibility: the form it takes under cultivation depends on the social groups in which we have lived. In the first place, it is necessary to live in numerous social groups and make many comparisons. In the second place, these must be groups for amusement and leisure, for in those that have to do with practical affairs it is interest and not pleasure that has to be considered. In the third place, there must not be too great inequality in the group and the tyranny of opinion must not be excessive: otherwise fashion stifles taste and people no longer desire what pleases but what gives distinction.

This matter of taste is one to which Emile cannot be indifferent in his present enquiries. The knowledge of what may be agreeable or disagreeable to men is essential to one who has need of them, and no less to one who wants to be useful to them. It is important to please people if you want to serve them.

If for the cultivation of my pupil's taste I had to make choice between a country in which culture has still to be developed and one in which it has already degenerated, I would begin his tour with the latter and finish with the former. The reason for this choice is that taste is spoiled by an over refinement which makes us sensitive to things which most people do not heed. This refinement introduces a spirit of discussion and increases the number of things that affect us. It makes for a subtlety which renders our intuitions more sensitive and less uniform, so that there come to be as many different tastes as there are people.

There is perhaps no civilised place on earth at the present time where the general taste is worse than in Paris. Yet it is in this capital that good taste can best be cultivated. There seem to be few books held in high esteem in Europe whose writers have not passed their formative years in Paris. Those who think it is enough to read these books are mistaken. There is more to be learned from the conversations of the authors than from their books; and it is not from the authors themselves that one learns most. It is the spirit of the community which develops a mind of power and widens the vision. If you have a spark of genius in you go and spend a year in Paris. You will soon reach the height of your powers, or you will come to nothing.

It is possible to learn to think in places where bad taste prevails, but there is no need to think like the people with bad taste, even if it is very difficult to avoid it when one is too long with them. It is necessary to perfect the instrument of judgment with their help, but to avoid using it as they do. Emile will go to Paris, but I will take care that his judgment does not get impaired in the refinement of it. When he has acquired an intuition delicate enough to appreciate and compare the diverse tastes of men, it is on the simplest objects I will lead him to fix his own taste.

Books and the Theatre (*The Value of the Classics*)

To keep his taste pure and healthy I will go still further. In the tumult of dissipation I will arrange to have useful conversations with him, and by directing the talk to topics that please him I will make these conversations both amusing and instructive. Now is the time to read agreeable books, and to teach him to analyse speech and appreciate all the beauties of eloquence and diction. Contrary to the general belief, there is little to be gained from the study of languages for themselves; but the study of languages leads to the study of the general principles of grammar. It is necessary to know Latin to get a proper knowledge of French. To learn the rules of the art of speech we must study and compare the two languages.

There is moreover a certain simplicity of taste that goes to the heart, which is to be found only in the writings of the ancients. In oratory, in poetry, in every kind of literature, the pupil will find them, as in history, abundant in matter and sober in judgment. In contrast with this our authors talk much and say little. To be always accepting their judgment as right is not the way to acquire a judgment of our own.

The difference between the two tastes makes itself felt in buildings and even on tombs. Our tombs are covered with eulogies: those of the ancients record facts. *Sta, viator. Heroem calcas* (Stop as you pass. Under your foot is a hero). If I had found this epitaph on an ancient monument I would have guessed immediately that it was modern, for nothing is so common as heroes among us whereas among the ancients they were rare. Instead of saying that a man was a hero they would have said what it was that made him one. They showed men as they were and made it plain that they were men. Xenophon doing honour to the memory of some soldiers slain by treason in the Retreat of the Ten Thousand says: 'They died, irreproachable in war and in friendship.' That is all, but note how full was the heart of the author of this short simple elegy. Only a miserable creature would not find it touch his own heart.

These words were engraved in marble at Thermopylae: 'Go, you that pass by, and tell Sparta that we died here in obedience to her holy laws.' It is evident that it was not the Academy of Inscriptions which composed that!

I will be much mistaken if my pupil who attaches little importance to words does not realise these differences at once and is not influenced by them in his choice of reading. He will be carried away by the masculine eloquence of Demosthenes and will say: 'This is an orator.' But on reading Cicero he will say: 'This is an advocate.'

Generally speaking Emile will have more liking for the writings of the ancients than our own, for the good reason that coming first they are nearer nature and their genius is more distinctive. Whatever may be said to the contrary the human reason shows no advance. What is gained in one direction is lost in another. All minds start from the same point, and the time spent in learning what others think is so much time lost for learning to think for ourselves. As time goes on there is more acquired knowledge and less vigour of mind.

It is not for the study of morals but of taste that I take Emile to the theatre, for it is there above all that taste reveals itself to thinking people. 'Give no thought to moral precepts,' I will say to him: 'it is not here that you will learn them.' The theatre is not intended to give truth but to humour and amuse. Nowhere can the art of pleasing men and touching the human heart be so well learned. The study of drama leads to the study of poetry: their object is the same. If Emile has even a glimmering of taste for poetry he will cultivate Greek, Latin and Italian —the languages of the poets—with great pleasure. The study of them will give him unlimited entertainment, and will profit him all the more on that account. They will bring him delight at an age and in circumstances when the heart finds charm in every kind of beauty. Imagine on the one hand my Emile, and, on the other, some young college scamp, reading the Fourth Book of the *Aeneid*, or Tibullus, or Plato's *Banquet*. What a difference there is: the heart of the one stirred to its depth by something that does not impress the other at all. Stop the reading, young man: you are too greatly moved. I want you to find pleasure in the language of love, but not to be carried away by it. Be' a man of feeling, but also a wise man. Actually, it is of no consequence whether Emile succeeds in the dead languages, in literature, in poetry or not. It would not matter greatly if he were ignorant of them all. His education is not really concerned with such diversions.

My main object in teaching him to feel and love beauty in every form is to fix his affections and his tastes on it and prevent his natural appetites from deteriorating so that he comes to look for the means of happiness in his wealth instead of finding it within himself. As I have said elsewhere, taste is simply the art of appreciating the little things, but since the pleasure of life depends on a multitude of little things such concern is not unimportant. It is by means of them that we come to enrich our lives with the good things at our disposal.

All this while we have been looking for Sophie but without finding her. It was important that she should not be found too quickly, and we have been looking for her where I was sure she would not be found. But now there is urgency. It is time to look for her in earnest, for fear Emile should mistake some one else for her and discover his mistake too late. Adieu then, Paris, city of fame and noise and smoke and dirt, where the women no longer believe in honour nor the men in virtue. Adieu, Paris. We are looking for love, happiness and innocence. We cannot get too far away from you.

BOOK FIVE

MARRIAGE

Editorial Note

There still remains one more task for the tutor before his work is complete. Having passed through his adolescence the young man must be prepared for the marriage which will make him a full member of the community. The story of Emile must therefore be halted till an account has been given of the education of the natural woman who is the only fit mate for the natural man. Sophie, destined to marry Emile, must be as typically woman as he is typically man. But before the romance can proceed on its sentimental journey an answer must be found for the question: what are the essential sex differences? These differences go deep in human nature, and the education which is to take account of this nature must be correspondingly different. Man is active and strong; woman passive and weak. Nature has therefore made the man the master, but his mastership is qualified by the need to please the woman, which gives her the compensating power to control and direct him. Each must get the education called for by personal and social functions so that they can play their proper parts in the man-woman relationship.

Having stated these basic principles Rousseau goes on to exemplify their educational implications in a delightful romance. Emile had to be brought up in his boyhood as if he were a kind of savage. Not so Sophie. She is just a simple country girl, preserved from the artifices of society by parents who themselves have turned their backs on town life and have directed her growing up in the spirit of freedom. The story might have ended with their meeting and their courtship, but no, they are still too young to marry and bring up a family. So Emile is sent off on his travels again, this time to study the problems of government as they present themselves in the nations of Europe, so that he may be equipped for intelligent citizenship when he becomes a citizen and head of a household.

The final task of the tutor is to instruct the young couple in their marital rights and duties. The book ends with the intimation that Emile intends to instruct the child-that-is-to-be himself and not to entrust him to a tutor. The father is the natural educator!

THE FINAL STAGE OF YOUTH

We have reached the last act in the drama of youth but the denouement has still to come.

It is not good for man to be alone. Emile is now a man. We must give him the mate we have promised him. The mate is Sophie. Once we know what kind of a person she is we will know better where to find her and we will be able to complete our task.

THE EDUCATION OF WOMEN

The Differences between the Sexes

Sophie should be as typically woman as Emile is man. She must possess all the characteristics of humanity and of womanhood which she needs for playing her part in the physical and the moral order. Let us begin by considering in what respects her sex and ours agree and differ.

In everything that does not relate to sex the woman is as the man: they are alike in organs, needs and capacities. In whatever way we look at them the difference is only one of less or more. In everything that relates to sex there are correspondences and differences. The difficulty is to determine what in their constitution is due to sex and what is not. All we know with certainty is that the common features are due to the species and the differences to sex. From this twofold point of view we find so many likenesses and so many contrasts that we cannot but marvel that nature has been able to create two beings so much alike with constitutions so different.

The sameness and the difference cannot but have an effect on mentality. This is borne out by experience and shows the futility of discussions about sex superiorities and inequalities. A perfect man and a perfect woman should no more resemble each other in mind than in countenance: and perfection does not admit of degrees.

In the mating of the sexes each contributes in equal measure to the common end but not in the same way. From this diversity comes the *first* difference which has to be noted in their personal relations. It is the part of the one to be active and strong, and of the other to be passive and weak. Accept this principle and it follows in the *second* place that woman is intended to please man. If the man requires to please the woman in turn the necessity is less direct. Masterfulness is his special attribute. He pleases by the very fact that he is strong. This is not the law of love, I admit. But it is the law of nature, which is more ancient than love.

If woman is made to please and to be dominated, she ought to make herself agreeable to man and avoid provocation. Her strength is in her charms and through them she should constrain him to discover his powers and make use of them. The surest way of bringing these powers into active operation is to make it necessary by her resistance. In this way self-esteem is added to desire and the man triumphs in the victory which the woman has compelled him to achieve. Out of this relation comes attack and defence, boldness on the one side and timidity on the other, and in the end the modesty and sense of shame with which nature has armed the weak for the subjugation of the strong.

Hence as a *third* consequence of the different constitution of the sexes, the stronger may appear to be master, and yet actually be dependent on the weaker: not because of a superficial practice of gallantry or the prideful generosity of the protective sex, but by reason of an enduring law of nature. By giving woman the capacity to stimulate desires greater than can be satisfied, nature has made man dependent on woman's good will and constrained him to seek to please her as a condition of her submission. Always there remains for man in his conquest the pleasing doubt whether strength has mastered weakness, or there has been a willing subjection; and the woman has usually the guile to leave the doubt unresolved.

Men and women are unequally affected by sex. The male is only a male at times; the female is a female all her life and can never forget her sex.

Plato in his *Republic* gives women the same physical training as men. That is what might be expected. Having made an end of private families in his state and not knowing what to do with the women, he found himself compelled to make men of them. That wonderful genius provided for everything in his plans, and went out of his way to meet an objection that nobody was likely to make, while missing the real objection. I am not speaking about the so-called community of wives, so often charged against him by people who have not read him. What I refer to is the social promiscuity which ignored the differences of sex by giving men and women the same occupations, and sacrificed the sweetest sentiments of nature to the artificial sentiment of loyalty which could not exist without them. He did not realise that the bonds of convention always develop from some natural attachment: that the love one has for his neighbours is the basis of his devotion to the state; that the heart is linked with the great fatherland through the little fatherland of the home; that it is the good son, the good husband, the good father, that makes the good citizen.

Differences in Education

Once it has been shown that men and women are essentially different in character and temperament, it follows that they ought not to have the same education. In accordance with the direction of nature they ought to co-operate in action, but not to do the same things. To complete the attempt we have been making to form the man of nature, we must now go on to consider how the fitting mate for him is to be formed.

If you want right guidance, always follow the leadings of nature. Everything that characterises sex should be respected as established by nature. Men's pride leads them astray when, comparing women with themselves, they say, as they are continually doing, that women have this or that defect, which is absent in men. What would be defects in men are good qualities in women, which are necessary to make things go on well. Women on their side never stop complaining that we men make coquettes of them and keep amusing them with trifles in order to maintain our ascendency. What a foolish idea! When have men ever had to do with the education of girls? Who prevents the mothers bringing up their daughters as they please? Are we men to blame if girls

please us by their beauty and attract us by the art they
have learned from their mothers? Well, try to educate
them like men. They will be quite willing. But the more
they resemble men the less will be their power over men,
and the greater their own subjection.

The faculties common to the sexes are not equally
shared between them; but take them all in all, they are
well balanced. The more womanly a woman is, the better.
Whenever she exercises her own proper powers she gains
by it: when she tries to usurp ours she becomes our
inferior. Believe me, wise mother, it is a mistake to bring
up your daughter to be like a good man. Make her a good
woman, and you can be sure that she will be worth more
for herself and for us. This does not mean that she should
be brought up in utter ignorance and confined to
domestic tasks. A man does not want to make his companion a servant and deprive himself of the peculiar
charms of her company. That is quite against the teaching
of nature, which has endowed women with quick pleasing
minds. Nature means them to think, to judge, to love, to
know and to cultivate the mind as well as the countenance. This is the equipment nature has given them to
compensate for their lack of strength and enable them to
direct the strength of men.

As I see it, the special functions of women, their
inclinations and their duties, combine to suggest the kind
of education they require. Men and women are made
for each other but they differ in the measure of their
dependence on each other. We could get on better
without women than women could get on without us.
To play their part in life they must have our willing help,
and for that they must earn our esteem. By the very law
of nature women are at the mercy of men's judgments
both for themselves and for their children. It is not

enough that they should be estimable: they must be esteemed. It is not enough that they should be beautiful: they must be pleasing. It is not enough that they should be wise: their wisdom must be recognised. Their honour does not rest on their conduct but on their reputation. Hence the kind of education they get should be the very opposite of men's in this respect. Public opinion is the tomb of a man's virtue but the throne of a woman's.

On the good constitution of the mothers depends that of the children and the early education of men is in their hands. On women too depend the morals, the passions, the tastes, the pleasures, aye and the happiness of men. For this reason their education must be wholly directed to their relations with men. To give them pleasure, to be useful to them, to win their love and esteem, to train them in their childhood, to care for them when they grow up, to give them counsel and consolation, to make life sweet and agreeable for them: these are the tasks of women in all times for which they should be trained from childhood.

TRAINING FOR WOMANHOOD
(1) TO THE AGE OF TEN

Physical Training for Grace

From the beginning little girls are fond of dress. Not content with being pretty they want notice taken of them. It is evident from their little airs that they have already got this concern. Almost as soon as they can understand what is said to them they can be controlled by telling them what people think of them. It would be foolish to speak that way to little boys and it would not have the same effect. Provided they are left free to enjoy their games boys care very little about what anybody thinks of them. It takes much time and effort to bring them under the same control.

However girls get this first lesson, it is a very good one. The body, one might say is born before the mind and for that reason must be trained first. That applies to both sexes but with a difference. In the boys the object of the training is the development of strength, in the girls the development of graces. Not that these qualities should be confined to one sex or the other but that they should differ in the importance attached to them. Women should have enough strength to do all they have to do gracefully: men enough skill to do what they have to do with ease.

Excessive softness in women makes men soft. They should not be sturdy like men but for them, so that they may be the mothers of sturdy males. From this point of view convents and boarding schools where the children get homely food and can run about and play freely in the open air and garden are preferable to the home where a delicately nurtured girl, always seated in a stuffy room under her mother's eye, dare not get up to walk or talk or breathe and is never free for a moment to jump or run or shout or give way to the natural petulance of her age. This is against all reason. It can only result in the ruin of both heart and body.

Everything that checks and constrains nature is in bad taste. This applies to the finery that bedecks the body as much as to the ornaments of the mind. Life, health, sanity, comfort ought to come first. There can be no grace without freedom and no charm in langour and illness. Suffering excites pity but it is the bloom of health that gives pleasure and delight.

*The Dressing of the Doll leading to Drawing, Counting,
Reading and Writing*

Children of the two sexes have many amusements in common, and that is right since it will be the same when they grow up. But they have also distinctive tastes. Boys like movement and noise: their toys are drums, tops and go-carts. Girls would rather have things that look well and serve for adornment: mirrors, jewels, dress materials and most of all dolls. The doll is the special plaything of the sex. Here the girl's liking is plainly directed towards her lifework. For her the art of pleasing finds its physical expression in dress. That is all a child can acquire of this art.

Look at the little girl, busy with her doll all day long, changing its trappings, dressing and undressing it hundreds of times, always on the outlook for new ways of decoration whether good or bad. Her fingers are clumsy and her taste unformed, but already her bent is evident. 'But,' you may say, 'she is dressing her doll, not herself.' No doubt! The fact is that she sees her doll and not herself. For the time being she herself does not matter. She is absorbed in the doll and her coquetry is expressed through it. But the time will come when she will be her own doll.

Here then right at the beginning is a well-marked taste. You have only to follow it up and give it direction. What the little one wishes most of all is to decorate her doll, to make bows, tippets, sashes, lacework for it. In all this she has to depend on the good will of others for help and it would be more convenient in every way if she could do it herself. Here is a motive for the first lessons given to her. They are not tasks prescribed for her but favours conferred. As a matter of fact nearly all little girls greatly dislike learning to read and write but they are always willing to learn to use the needle. They imagine themselves grown up and think happily of the time when they will be using their talents in adorning themselves.

This first open road is easy to follow. Tapestry which is the amusement of women is not much to the liking of girls, and furnishings, having nothing to do with the person, are remote from their interests. But needlework, embroidery and lacemaking come readily to them. The same willing progress leads on easily to drawing, for this art is not unrelated to that of dressing one's self with good taste. I would not have girls taught to draw landscape or to do figure painting. It will be enough if they draw leaves, flowers, fruit, draperies, anything that can add to the elegance of dress and enable them to make their own embroidery patterns. If it is important for men to confine their studies in the main to everyday knowledge, it is even more important for women whose way of life, though less laborious, does not permit them to devote themselves to the talent of their choice at the expense of their duties.

Whatever the humorists may say, good sense is common to the two sexes. Girls are generally more docile than boys and in any case have more need to be brought under authority. But this does not mean that they should be required to do things without seeing the use of them. The maternal art is to make evident the purpose of everything that is prescribed to them; and this is all the easier to do since the girl's intelligence is more precocious than the boy's. This principle excludes for both boys and girls not only studies which serve no obvious purpose but even those which only become useful at a later stage. If it is wrong to urge a boy to learn to read it is even worse to compel little girls to do so before making them realise the value of reading. After all what need have girls to read and write at an early age? They are not going to have a household to manage for a long time to come. All of them have curiosity enough to make sure that they will learn without compulsion when leisure and the occasion come. Possibly they should learn to count first of all. Counting has an obvious utility at all stages and much practice is required to avoid errors in calculation. I guarantee that if a little girl does not get cherries at tea-time till she has performed some arithmetical exercise she will very soon learn to count.

The Prevention of Idleness and Indocility

Always justify the tasks you impose on young girls but impose them all the same. Idleness and indocility are their most dangerous faults and are most difficult to cure once they are contracted. Not only should girls be careful and industrious but they should be kept under control from an early age. This hardship, if it be a hardship, is inseparable from their sex. All their lives they will be under the hard, unceasing constraints of the proprieties. They must be disciplined to endure them till they come to take them as a matter of course and learn to overcome caprice and bow to authority. If they are inclined to be always busy they should sometimes be compelled to do nothing whatever. To save them from dissipation, caprice and fickleness they must learn above all to master themselves.

Do not let girls get bored with their occupations and turn too keen on their amusements, as happens in the ordinary education where, as Fénelon says, all the boredom is on the one side and all the pleasure on the other. A girl will only be bored with her tasks if she gets on badly with the people around her. A little one who loves her mother or some darling friend will work in their company day in day out and never become tired. The constraint put on the child, so far from weakening the affection she has for her mother, will make it stronger; for dependence is a state natural to women, and girls realise that they are made for obedience.

And just because they have, or ought to have, little freedom, they carry the freedom they have to excess. Extreme in all things, they devote themselves to their play with greater zeal than boys. This is the second defect. This zeal must be kept within bounds. It is the cause of several vices peculiar to women, among others the capricious changing of their tastes from day to day. Do not deprive them of mirth, laughter, noise and romping games, but prevent them tiring of one game and turning to another. They must get used to being stopped in the middle of their play and put to other tasks without protest on their part. This daily constraint will produce the docility that women need all their lives. The first and most important quality of a woman is sweetness. Being destined to obey a being so imperfect as man (often with many vices and always with many shortcomings), she must learn to submit uncomplainingly to unjust treatment and marital wrongs. Not for his sake but for her own she must preserve her sweetness.

Girls should always be submissive, but mothers should not always be inexorable. To make a young person docile there is no call to make her unhappy. Indeed I should not be sorry if sometimes she were allowed to exercise a little cunning, not to elude punishment but to escape having to obey. Guile is a natural gift of her sex; and being convinced that all natural dispositions are good and right in themselves I think that this one should be cultivated like the rest. The characteristic cunning with which women are endowed is an equitable compensation for their lesser strength. Without it women would not be the comrade of man but his slave. This talent gives her the superiority that keeps her his equal and enables her to rule him even while she obeys.

TRAINING FOR WOMANHOOD
(2) AFTER THE AGE OF TEN

Adornment and the Arts of Pleasing

Fine dress may make a woman outstanding, but it is only the person herself that pleases. The attire that is least noticeable often makes its wearer most noticed. The education of young girls in this respect is utterly wrong. They are promised ornaments for rewards, and taught to love gorgeous apparel. 'How beautiful she is,' people say when a girl is all dressed up. This is quite wrong. Girls should learn that so much finery is only put on to hide defects, and that the triumph of beauty is to shine by itself. If I saw a young girl strutting like a peacock in gay garments I should show myself disturbed by this disguising of her figure. I should remark: 'What a pity she is so over-dressed. Do you not think she could do with something simpler? Is she pretty enough to dispense with this or that?' Perhaps she would then be the first to want the ornamentation removed so that she might be judged on her merits.

The first thing that young persons notice as they grow up is that external adornment is not enough, if they lack accomplishments of their own. They cannot make themselves beautiful, and it is too soon for them to play the coquette; but they are old enough to have graceful gestures, an attractive accent, a self-possessed bearing, a light step, and gracious manners. At this stage the voice improves in range, strength and tone, the arms develop, the movements become more confident; and with all this comes the discovery that there is an art by which they can win attention in any situation. From this point sewing and industry no longer suffice of themselves. New talents make their appearance and their usefulness is recognised.

I know that austere teachers are against teaching girls singing or dancing or any of the arts of pleasing. Secular songs, they say, are wicked. Dancing is an invention of the devil. A young girl should find entertainment enough in work and prayer. Strange entertainments these for a child of ten! For my part I greatly fear that the little saints who have been compelled to spend their childhood in prayer will occupy their youth in quite different ways and make up for what they missed in girlhood when they marry. We should consider what befits age as well as befits sex. A young girl should not live like her grandmother. She should be lively and merry. She should dance and sing as much as she likes and enjoy all the innocent pleasures of her age.

The agreeable accomplishments have been made too formal with maxims and precepts, and what ought to be only light-hearted games have been made burdensome for young people. Take music, for example. Is written music really necessary? Is it not possible to make the voice flexible and true and to teach expressive singing without the knowledge of a single note? Is the same kind of song suitable for all voices? Does the same method suit every temperament? I just do not believe that the same poses, steps, gestures, dances can befit a lively little brunette and a big blonde beauty with languishing eyes. So when I see a teacher giving the same lessons to two such people I say:

'The man is following a routine. He knows nothing of his art.'

The question is sometimes raised whether girls should be taught by masters or mistresses. Personally I would rather they had no need for either but should learn of themselves what they are strongly inclined to learn. In the arts which have pleasure as their object anyone can teach a young girl—father or mother, sister or brother, girl friends, governesses, her mirror, above all her own taste. Taste is formed by industry and the natural gifts. By its means the mind is gradually opened to the idea of beauty in all its forms, and ultimately to those moral notions allied to beauty. This is perhaps one reason why the sentiments of decency and propriety are acquired by girls sooner than by boys. They certainly do not come from their governesses.

The art of speech takes first place among the pleasing arts. It is the mind with its succession of feelings and ideas that imparts life and variety to the countenance and inspires the talk that keeps the attention fixed on one object. That, I believe, is why young girls so quickly learn to chatter agreeably and put expression into their talk, even before they feel it. And that is why men find it amusing to listen to them so soon: they are waiting for the first gleam of intelligence to break through feeling.

The chatter of girls should not be curbed by the hard question that one puts to boys: 'What's the good of that?' but rather by the other question that is no more easy to answer: 'What will be the effect of that?' In the early years before they can distinguish good and evil, or pass judgment on other people, girls should make it a rule for themselves to say only agreeable things to those with whom they are talking. What makes this rule difficult in

practice is that it must always be kept subordinate to our
first rule: 'Never tell a lie.'

Religion

It is obvious that if male children cannot form any true
idea of religion it is still more beyond the comprehension
of girls. For that very reason I would speak to them about
it at an earlier age, for if it were necessary to wait till
they were able to discuss these profound questions the
chances are that they would never be mentioned at all.
Just as a woman's conduct is subject to public opinion, so
is her faith subject to authority. Every girl should have
her mother's religion, and every woman her husband's.
Not being able to judge for themselves in such matters,
they should accept the conviction of fathers and husbands
as they accept that of the church.

The important thing in teaching religion to young girls
is not to make it doleful or boring. It should not be
either a task or a duty. For that reason never make them
learn anything that has to do with it by heart, not even
their prayers. Be content to say your own prayers
regularly in their presence, but do not compel them to
take any part in them. Following the instructions of Jesus
Christ, make prayers short and always say them with
becoming reverence.

It is of less consequence that girls should learn their
religion young than that they should learn it well and still
more that they should love it. If you make it onerous and
are always depicting God as angry with them, if in His
name you impose on them a great many disagreeable
duties which they never see you fulfil yourself, what can
they think but that learning the catechism and praying
to God are duties for little girls and will wish to be grown

up like you to escape this obligation? Example is all important. Without it you will never make any impression on children.

When you explain the articles of faith let it be in the form of direct instruction and not by question and answer. Girls should only answer what they think themselves and not what has been prescribed for them. The answers in the catechism are all topsy-turvy: it is the scholar who instructs the teacher. In the mouths of children, indeed, the answers are lies since they are required to explain what they cannot understand and make affirmations that as yet they cannot possibly believe.

The question that comes first in our catechism is this: 'Who created you and brought you into the world?' To this the little girl, though knowing quite well that it was her mother, replies without hesitation that it was God. I wish a man well acquainted with the growing mind of children would make a catechism for them. With such a catechism the child would have to give his own untutored replies and be at liberty to ask questions in his turn. To illustrate what I mean, let me give by way of example the kind of question I imagine might lead up to the first question of our catechism:

NURSE: Do you remember the time when your mother was a little girl?

CHILD: No. N.: Why not, with your good memory? CH.: I was not in the world then. N.: Then you were not always alive? CH.: No. N.: Will you live for ever? CH.: Oh, yes. N.: Are you young or old? CH.: I am young. N.: And your grandma—is she young or old? . . . Will you grow old like her? CH.: I do not know . . . N.: And what becomes of old people? CH.: I do not know. N.: What became of your grandpapa? CH.: He is dead. N.: And why he is dead? CH.: Because he was old. N.: What becomes of old people then? CH.: They die. N.: And what about you when you turn old? CH.: Oh nurse I don't want to die . . .

The questions go on till the discovery is made that for the human race as for everything else in the world there is a beginning and an end: at the one extreme, a father and a mother without father and mother, at the other extreme, children who will have no children. And so after a long succession of questions the child is ready for the first question in the catechism. But between that and the reply to the second question concerning the divine essence is a very great gap. *God is a spirit*. Aye, but what is a spirit? These metaphysical questions are not for a little girl to answer. She might indeed raise them. In that case I would answer simply: 'You ask me what is God. That is not an easy question to answer. We cannot hear, or see, or touch God. We only know Him by His works. To judge what He is, you must wait till you know what He has done.'

Pass over all those mysterious doctrines, which are mere words for us. Keep children within the narrow circle of doctrines that have to do with morality, and make them understand that the only things worth our knowing are those that teach us to live good lives. Don't make your girls theologians and dialecticians. Accustom them to feel themselves always under the eyes of God, and to live as they will be glad to have lived when they appear before Him. That is the true religion, the only one incapable of abuse, impiety or fanaticism. I know no better.

The Training of Reason

It is well to keep in mind that up to the age when reason becomes active and the growth of sentiment makes conscience speak, good or bad for young women is only what those around them so regard. What they are told to do is good: what they are forbidden is bad. That is all they have to know. From this it is evident how important is the choice of those who are to be with them and exercise authority over them, even more than in the case of boys. But in due course the moment will come when they begin to form their own judgment and then the plan of their education must be changed. We cannot leave them with social prejudices as the only law of their lives. For all human beings there is a rule of conduct which comes before public opinion. All other rules are subject to the inflexible direction of this rule. Even prejudices must be judged by it, and it is only in so far as the values of men are in accord with it that they are entitled to have authority over us. This rule is conscience, the inner conviction (*sentiment*). Unless the two rules are in concord in women's education, it is bound to be defective. Personal conviction without regard for public opinion will fail to give them that fineness of soul which puts the hallmark of worldly honour on good conduct; and public opinion lacking personal conviction will only make false, dishonest women with a sham virtue. For the co-ordination of the two guides to right living, women need to cultivate a faculty to arbitrate between them, to prevent conscience going astray on the one hand and correct the errors of prejudice on the other. This faculty is reason. But at the mention of reason all sorts of questions arise. Are women capable of sound reasoning? Is it necessary for them to cultivate it? If they do cultivate it, will it be of any use to them in the functions imposed on them? Is it compatible with a becoming simplicity?

The reason that brings a man to a knowledge of his duties is not very complex. The reason that brings a woman to hers is simpler still. The obedience and loyalty she owes to her husband and the tender care she owes her children are such obvious and natural consequences of her position that she cannot without bad faith refuse to listen to the inner sentiment which is her guide, nor fail to recognise her duty in her natural inclination. Since she depends on her own conscience and on the opinion of other people she must learn to compare and harmonise the two rules. This can best be done by cultivating her understanding and her reason.

SOPHIE

The Outcome of the Right Education

Let us now look at the picture of Sophie which has been put before Emile, the image he has of the woman who can make him happy.

Sophie is well born and has a good natural disposition. She has a feeling heart which sometimes makes her imagination difficult to control. Her mind is acute rather than precise: her temper easy but variable; her person ordinary but pleasing. Her countenance gives indication of a soul—with truth. Some girls have good qualities she lacks and others have the qualities she possesses in fuller measure; but none has these qualities better combined in a happy character. Without being very striking, she interests and charms, and it is difficult to say why.

Sophie is fond of dress and has taste enough to dress well. She dislikes rich clothes and her own always combine simplicity with elegance. She does not know which are the fashionable colours, but she knows to perfection those that suit herself. No girl gives less sign of careful dressing and yet no piece of hers has been selected casually. Her dress is modest in appearance but coquettish in effect.

She does not display her charms, but hides them in such a way as to appeal to the imagination.

Sophie has natural talents. She is aware of them and has not neglected them. But not having been in a position to give much thought to their cultivation, she has been content to exercise her sweet voice in singing with truth and taste, and her little feet in walking with an easy grace. She has had no singing teacher but her father, and no dancing mistress but her mother. A neighbouring organist has given her a few lessons in playing accompaniments on the harpsichord, which she has practised alone. But music for her is a taste rather than a talent, and she cannot play a tune by note.

What Sophie knows best and has been most carefully taught are the tasks of her own sex, even those like dressmaking, not usually thought necessary. There is no kind of needlework she cannot do, but she has a special preference for lace-making because it calls for a pleasing pose, as well as grace and lightness in the fingers. She has also applied herself to all the details of the household. She understands cookery and kitchen work. She knows the prices of provisions and can judge their qualities. She can keep accounts and is her mother's housekeeper. At the same time, she does not take equal pleasure in all her duties. For example, though she likes nice food she is not fond of cooking, and is rather disgusted with some of its details. For the same reason she has always been unwilling to inspect the garden. The soil seems to her dirty, and when she sees the dunghill she imagines she feels a smell. This defect she owes to her mother, according to whom cleanliness is one of the first obligations imposed on a woman by nature. The result is that cleaning takes up an undue amount of Sophie's time.

Sophie's mind is pleasing but not brilliant, solid but

not deep. She has always something attractive to say to those who talk with her, but lacks the conversational adornments we associate with cultured women. Her mind has been formed, not only by reading but by conversation with her father and mother and by her own reflections on the little bit of the world she has seen. She is too sensitive to preserve a perfect evenness of temper, but too sweet to allow this to be troublesome to other people. It is only herself that is hurt.

She is religious, but her religion is reasonable and simple, with few dogmas and still fewer observances. The essential observance for her is morality, and she devotes her life to the service of God by doing good. In all the instructions they have given her on this subject her parents have accustomed her to a respectful submission. 'My daughter,' they say to her, 'this knowledge is not for one of your age. When the time comes your husband will instruct you.' Apart from that, they are content to dispense with long pious talks, and only preach to her by their example.

The love of virtue is her ruling passion. She loves virtue, because it is the glory of a woman and the only road to true happiness; because, also, it is dear to her respected father and her tender mother. These sentiments inspire her with an enthusiasm that uplifts the soul and keeps all her young inclinations in subjection to the noble passion for virtue. She will be chaste and good till her last breath. She has sworn it in the depths of her soul.

As well developed in all respects as a girl of twenty, Sophie at the age of fifteen will not be treated as a child by her parents. As soon as they perceive in her the first unquiet of youth they will hasten to anticipate its further progress. They will have tender, judicious talks with her, suited to her age and character. Her father, it may be supposed, will talk to her at considerable length about marriage and all that it means for her.

'I propose an agreement,' he will say in conclusion, 'which shows our esteem for you, and re-establishes the natural order between you and us. The custom is that parents choose their daughter's husband and only consult her as a matter of form. We will follow the opposite course. You will choose and we shall be consulted. Exercise your right freely and wisely, Sophie. The husband best fitted for you should be your choice, and not ours. But it is for us to judge whether you have not been mistaken about his suitability and whether, without knowing it, you are not doing something you do not intend. Birth, wealth, rank, conventions will not enter our minds. Select a good man of pleasing personality and fitting character, and we will accept him as our son-in-law.'

Sophie's Ideal Man: Telemachus

May I venture to go straight ahead with the story of a girl so like Sophie that nobody would be surprised to learn that this story was hers? This young girl so resembles Sophie in all respects, that we may continue to call her by the name she is worthy to bear. After the conversation I have related, her father and mother, thinking that suitable husbands were not likely to present themselves in the hamlet in which they lived, sent her to spend the winter in town with an aunt who had been secretly acquainted with the purpose of the journey. This aunt introduced her to people, took her into company, showed her the world, or rather showed her to the world. It was noticeable that she did not keep out of the way of young men of comely appearance who were decent and modest, but that she never gave them the chance to do her the least service: indicating in this way that she did not wish to be their mistress. Not finding what she had gone to look for, she grew tired of the town life, and returned home long before the time fixed for her return.

Scarcely had she resumed her duties in the paternal home when it was seen that she was distracted, impatient, melancholy and dreamy. At first her parents thought that she was in love and was ashamed of it, but she denied this, protesting that she had never yet seen anyone who could touch her heart. Her mother invited her confidence. Why was she not using the freedom she had been given? Why had she not chosen a husband? 'How unhappy I am,' she said. 'I want to be loved, but I see no one who pleases me. I would rather die unhappy but free, than be driven to despair by the company of a man I do not love.' The mother suspecting some mystery urged her to speak. Leaving the room Sophie came back a moment after with a book in her hand: it was Fénelon's romance, *The Adventure of Telemachus*.

Sophie loved Telemachus with a passion nothing could cure. 'Does the heart depend on the will?' she asked. 'Is it my fault if I love someone who does not exist? I am not looking for a prince like Telemachus. I know he is only a story book character, but I am looking for someone like him. And why should this someone not exist, seeing that I who am conscious of a heart like his exist? Perhaps there is such a man and he is looking for me. But who he is and where he is, I do not know.'

EMILE AND SOPHIE

Let us give Emile his Sophie. Let us bring this sweet girl to life, but with a less active imagination and a happier fate. A pupil of nature like Emile, she is better suited for him than any other woman. She is indeed his woman, his equal in birth and merit, his inferior in fortune. Her special charm only reveals itself gradually, as one comes to know her, and her husband will appreciate it more than anyone. Her education is in no way exceptional. She has taste without study, talents without art, judgment without knowledge. Her mind is still vacant but has been trained to learn: it is well-tilled land only waiting for the grain. What a pleasing ignorance! Happy is the man destined to instruct her. She will be her husband's disciple, not his teacher. Far from wanting to impose her tastes on him, she will share his. It is time they met.

Emile and I set off from Paris in melancholy mood, busy with our thoughts. This place of talk is not our centre. Emile looks disdainfully on the great city, and says with vexation: 'What a waste of time on a vain search. That is not where the spouse of my heart would be.' Well, here we are in the country, journeying not like couriers but like explorers. We are not thinking merely of the beginning and the end of the journey, but of what lies between. The journey itself is a pleasure for us. We do not travel imprisoned in a small tightly shut cage, deprived of the fresh air or the sight of things around us that may happen to please us. Emile never enters a post chaise or rides post unless he is in a hurry. And what would make him hurry in any case? Only the joy of life.

I can only think of one way of travelling more agreeable than riding, and that is to go on foot. You start and you stop when you will. You take as much or as little exercise as you care. You see the whole countryside. You turn off to the right, or the left. You examine anything you fancy. You stop at every point that commands a view.

If I see a stream I go along the edge: if a leafy wood, I go under its shade: if a cave, I visit it: if a quarry, I examine the minerals. I rest wherever I please, and when I am bored I move on. I am independent of horses or postillion. I do not need to choose made roads or the usual routes. As I depend only on myself I enjoy all the liberty a man can. To travel on foot is to travel like Thales, Plato and Pythagoras. It is difficult to understand how a philosopher could allow himself to travel any other way. Surely anyone who is even a little fond of agriculture wants to know the special products of the places through which he is passing. Can anyone with a little taste for natural history pass through a bit of country without examining it, or go past a rock without chipping off a piece, or climb over hills without botanising? Your urban scientists study natural history in cabinets. They have snippets of things, of which they know the names but not the nature. But Emile's cabinet is richer than those of kings for his is the whole earth. Everything has a place of its own in it. The Great Naturalist who looks after it has arranged it all in the finest order.

How many different delights we gain by this agreeable way of travelling, not reckoning improving health and a cheery mood. How lightsome of heart we are as we approach our lodging! How savoury even a coarse meal tastes! With what pleasure we slack off at table. If you only want to go somewhere, go by post chaise, but if you want to travel you must go by foot.

We always keep moving on. One day after we had wandered further than usual in the trackless hill country we lost our way. Fortunately we met a peasant who took us to his house, where we enjoyed a meagre dinner. 'If the good God had led you to the other side of the hill,' he said, 'you would have got a better reception. You would have found a house of peace where dwell good kindly people.' Off we set for this house early next day but did not reach it till the evening. We were received hospitably and shown into a small clean well-furnished room with a fire and every comfort. 'Why,' cried Emile in surprise, 'you would think we had been expected. What kindness. What forethought for strangers. I could almost believe that we are in the times of Homer.' Having dried ourselves and made ourselves tidy we rejoined the master of the house and were presented by him to his wife. The honour of her glances was for Emile. A mother in her situation rarely sees a young man come into the house without anxiety or at least without curiosity.

Dinner was hurried on for our sake. There were five places set but one remained empty. Then a young girl entered, made a deep curtsy and sat down modestly without saying a word. Emile, occupied with his hunger and the conversation, bowed to her and went on eating and talking. A casual reference to Telemachus threw the girl into deep confusion. 'Sophie,' said the mother, 'control yourself.' Emile hearing the name Sophie looked at her, wondering if this was to be his mate and immediately fell in love with her. Sophie has found Telemachus.

If I go into the simple, unsophisticated story of their innocent love I will be considered frivolous, but that is a mistake. Not sufficient consideration is given to the influence of the first relations of man and woman on the whole course of the future lives of both. People do not realise the lasting effect of an experience so vivid as the first love, throughout the years, on to death. We are given in educational treatises long wordy discourses on the imaginery duties of children, but not a word is spoken about the most important and most difficult part of their education, the crisis which marks the transition from child to adult. If I have been specially helpful in this book it will be because I have dealt at length with this essential matter which others omit, and have not allowed myself to be diverted from this enterprise by false delicacy, or the difficulty of finding fitting language.

Once he is Sophie's accepted lover and has become really anxious to please her, Emile begins to realise the value of the agreeable talents which he has acquired. Sophie is fond of singing. He sings with her: more than that, he teaches her music. She is lively and nimble and is fond of skipping. He dances with her and changes her steps into perfect dance movements. These lessons are charming and are inspired by a light-hearted gaiety. It is right for a lover to be the master of his mistress.

There is an old harpsichord which is in very bad condition. Emile mends it and puts it in tune. It has always been his rule to learn to do everything he can for himself, where possible: he is an instrument maker and mender as well as a carpenter. The house is in a picturesque situation. He makes various drawings of it with some help from Sophie, for her father's room. When she sees Emile drawing she imitates him and improves her own drawing. She cultivates all her talents, and her charm embellishes them.

It is both touching and funny to see. Emile bent on teaching Sophie everything he knows, regardless of whether she wants to learn or whether it is suitable for her. He talks to her about everything, and explains things with boyish eagerness. He assumes that he has only to talk and immediately she will listen. He looks forward to discussing things with her and regards everything he has learned which cannot be told to her as of no account. He almost blushes at the thought of knowing something she does not know.

Here then is Emile teaching her philosophy, physics, mathematics, history, everything in fact. She lends herself with pleasure to his zeal, and tries to profit by it. The art of thinking is not alien to women, but they only need a nodding acquaintance with logic and metaphysics. Sophie forms some idea of everything, but most of what she learns is soon forgotten. She makes best progress in matters of conduct and taste. In the case of physics she has only a limited idea of the general laws and system of the universe. Sometimes when the pair contemplate the wonders of nature in the course of their walks their pure and innocent hearts seek to rise to its Author and they fearlessly pour out their hearts before Him together.

My young man is far from passing his whole time with Sophie. He is only allowed to visit her once or twice a week, and his visits rarely extend to the next day and are often only for the half day. On the days he does not see her he does not stay idle indoors: he is still the old Emile. Most often he wanders over the countryside, interested in its natural history. He observes and examines the products and tillage of the land in different districts. He compares the methods he sees with those he knows, and looks for an explanation of the differences. If he thinks other methods are better than those in use he brings them to the notice of the farmers. If he has a better kind of plough to suggest, he gets one made from his own drawings. If he finds a lime quarry, he teaches them the use of lime, which they do not know. Often he puts his own hand to the job, and they are astonished to see him handling all their tools better than they can themselves. They do not scoff at him for fine talk about agriculture. They see that he knows about it at first hand. In a word, he extends his zeal and care to everything of immediate and general utility.

But he does not confine himself to that. He visits the homes of the peasants, finds out about their circumstances, their families, the number of their children, the extent of their land, what they produce, their markets, their privileges, their taxes, their debts, and so on. He rarely gives them money, unless he can control the use of it himself. For one he gets the house that is falling to ruin repaired or thatched. For another he has the ground which has been abandoned for lack of means cleaned up. For another he provides a cow, a horse or other stock to replace a loss. He reconciles two neighbours who are on the point of going to law. He gets attention for a sick peasant and makes sure that he has proper food and drink. He helps poor young people who want to get married. He never despises the poor and unfortunate. He often takes a meal with the peasants he is helping. He is the benefactor of some, and the friend of others, but he never ceases to be their equal. To sum up everything, he always does as much good in person as with his money.

Along with these various occupations there is also the trade we have learned. At least one day a week, and twice when the weather is bad, Emile and I go to work for a master, like regular workmen. Sophie's father found us busy at work when he came to see us and did not fail to report with admiration to his wife and daughter what he had seen. They decided to surprise Emile at his work. Entering the workshop Sophie finds a young man in a jacket, with untidy hair, so intent on what he is doing that he does not see her. Emile, chisel in one hand and mallet in the other is finishing a mortise: then he saws a plank and clamps down a board to polish it. This sight does not amuse Sophie. It touches her and wins her respect. Women, honour your master. It is he who works for you, and earns the bread that feeds you. This is your man.

Later Emile and Sophie go to a peasant home where the father has had his leg broken, the mother has a new born babe, and there are two young children. Sophie, ignoring dirt and smells, puts the house in order and makes both invalids comfortable. Emile looking on is greatly touched. Man, love your mate. God has given her to you to lighten your sorrows and comfort you in your misfortunes. This is your woman.

EMILE ON HIS TRAVELS

The Control of Affection

One morning when they had not seen each other for two days I went into Emile's room with a letter in my hand. Looking at him fixedly, I said: 'What would you do if some one were to inform you that Sophie is dead?' He gave a loud cry, sprang up and struck his hands, and without a word looked at me with haggard eyes. 'Reassure yourself,' I said; 'she is alive and well, and we are expected tonight. Let us go for a short stroll and we can talk things over. We must be happy, dear Emile,' I said. 'Happiness is the end of every sentient being. It is the first desire impressed on us by nature and the only one that never leaves us. But where is happiness to be found? Nobody knows. Everybody seeks it: nobody finds it. All through life we pursue it, but die without attaining it. If you want to live happily fix your heart on the beauty that never perishes. Let your desires be limited by your condition in life and put your duties before your inclinations. Extend the law of necessity into the sphere of morals and learn to lose whatever can be taken from you, and to rise above the chances of life. Then you will be happy in spite of fortune and wise in spite of passion. In the good things that are most fragile you will find a pleasure that nothing can disturb. They will not possess you but you will possess them; and you will discover that in this passing world man only enjoys what he is ready to give up. You will not have the illusion of imaginary pleasures, it is true, but neither will you suffer the sorrows that attend them. When you no longer attach an undue importance to life you will pass your own life untroubled and come to the end of it without fear. Others, terror-stricken, may believe that when death comes they will cease to be. You, being aware of the nothingness of this life, will know that the real life is just beginning.'

Emile listened with anxious attention. He foresaw the hard discipline to which I had it in mind to subject him. 'What must I do?' he asked, with eyes downcast. 'You must leave Sophie. Sophie is not yet eighteen and you are barely twenty-two. This is the age for love but not for marriage. You are too young to be the father and mother of a family. Do you not know how premature motherhood can weaken the constitution, ruin the health and shorten the life of young women? When mother and child are both growing and the substance needed for the growth of each of them has to be shared between the two, neither get what nature meant them to get. As for yourself, have you given proper thought to the duties you undertake when you become a husband and a father? When you become the head of a family you become a member of the state. Do you know what that involves? You have studied the duties of a man but do you know what the duties of a citizen are? Do you know what is meant by "government," "laws," "country"? Do you know the price that has to be paid for life and the causes for which you must be ready to die? Before entering the civil order seek to realise and understand what is your proper place in it.'

Emile stood silent for a moment, then looked at me steadily: 'When do we start?' he said. 'In a week's time,' I replied. Sophie I consoled and reassured. Let her keep faith with him as he would with her, and I swear that they will be married in two years' time.

The Educational Value of Travel

The question is much discussed whether it is good for young people to travel. A better way of putting it would be to ask whether it is enough for an educated man to know only his own countrymen. For my part I am firmly convinced that anyone who only knows the people among whom he lives does not know mankind. But even admitting the utility of travel, does it follow that it is good for everybody? Far from it. It is only good for the few people who are strong enough in themselves to listen to the voice of error and not let themselves be seduced, and see examples of vice and not be led astray. Travel develops the natural bent and makes a man either good or bad. More come back bad than good because more start off with an inclination to badness. But those who are well born and have a good nature which has been well trained, those who travel with a definite purpose of learning, all come back better than they went away. That applies to my Emile.

Everything done rationally should have its rules. This holds good for travel, considered as a part of education. To travel merely for the sake of travelling is to wander about like a vagabond. Even to travel for instruction is too vague a matter. A journey without some definite aim is of no use. I would give a young man an obvious interest in learning, and this interest (if well chosen) would in turn fix the nature of the instruction. After he has considered his physical relations with the world and his moral relations with other men, it remains for him to consider his civic relations with his compatriots. For this he must study the nature of government in general, then the different forms of government, and finally the particular government under which he has been born, in order to know whether it is the one suited for him. By a right which nothing can annul, every man when he reaches his majority and becomes his own master is entitled to renounce the contract by which he is bound to the community and leave the country of his birth. It is only by staying on in that country after coming to the age of reason that he is judged to confirm tacitly the engagement made by his ancestors. Yet the place of his birth being a gift of nature, he gives up something of his own if he renounces it.

Here is what I would say to Emile. 'Up to this time you have not been your own master but have lived under my direction. You are coming to the age when the law allows you the control of your property and makes you master of your person. You have in mind establishing a household of your own, and that is as it should be: it is one of the duties of a man. But before you marry you must know what kind of man you want to be, how you mean to spend your life, what measures you are going to take to ensure a living for yourself and your family. Are you willing to depend on men you despise? Are you willing to have your fortune and your social position determined by civil relations which will subject you for all time to the discretion of other people?' Next, I would describe to him all the different ways of turning his possessions to account in commerce, in public office, in finance, and show him that in every case his position would be precarious and dependent. There is another way of employing his time and himself, I would tell him. You can join the army and hire yourself out at a very high rate to go and kill people who never did you any harm. But far from making you independent of other resources, this job only makes them more necessary for you.

It may be surmised that none of these occupations will be greatly to Emile's taste. 'Do you think I have forgotten the games of my childhood,' he will say to me. 'Have I lost my arms? Has my strength failed? Can I no longer work? All the property I want is a little farm in some corner of the world. My only ambition will be to work it and live free from worry. With Sophie and my land I will be rich.' 'You speak of your own land, dear Emile. But where are you going to find it? In what corner to the earth can you say: "I am my own master and master of the ground I occupy?" There are places where a man can become rich: none where he can spend his life without riches. Nowhere is it possible to live a free and independent life, doing ill to no one, fearing ill from no one. Your plan, Emile, is a fine one and an honourable one, and it would certainly bring you happiness. Let us do our best to realise it. I have a proposal to make. Let us devote the two years till you are due to return to Sophie to looking for a place of refuge somewhere in Europe where you can live happily with your family, secure from danger. If we succeed you will have found the happiness which is sought in vain by so many others. If we do not succeed, you will be cured of an illusion. You will console yourself for an unavoidable evil, and submit to the law of necessity.'

The time has come to draw to an end. We must bring Emile back to Sophie. We have spent almost two years going through some of the great states of Europe and many of the small ones. We have learned two or three of the chief languages. We have seen the unusual things in natural history, government, arts and men. Emile, consumed with impatience, calls my attention to the fact that the time is nearly up. Then I say to him: 'Well, my friend, you remember the main object of our travels. What conclusions have you reached after all your observations?' Unless I have been wrong in my method he will answer something like this: 'What conclusion? To remain the kind of person you have trained me to be, and not to add by my own will any bonds to those which nature and the laws have put on me. The more I examine the work of men in their institutions, the more I see that in seeking independence they make themselves slaves. To avoid being carried away by the torrent of things they form a thousand attachments: then when they try to take a step forward they are surprised to find themselves being held back. It seems to me that the way to become free is just to do nothing, and give up trying to be free. You yourself, master, have made me free by teaching me to yield to necessity. What matters the fortune left me by my parents? I will begin by not depending on it. If I am allowed I will keep it: if it is taken from me I will not let myself be carried away with it. Rich or poor I will be free. What does my earthly condition matter? Wherever there are men I am among brothers: where there are none I have still my own home. If my belongings enslave me I will give them up without hesitation. I can work for my living. Whatever time death comes I will defy it. Having accepted things as they are I will never need to struggle against destiny. There is one and only one chain I shall always wear, and in that I will glory. Give me Sophie, and I am free.'

'My dear Emile,' I reply, 'I am very pleased to hear

you speak like a man. Before you set out on your travels I knew what the outcome would be. I knew that when you made acquaintance with our institutions you would not be tempted to put greater confidence in them than they deserve. Men vainly aspire to freedom under safeguard of the laws. Liberty is not to be found in any form of government. It is in the heart of the free man. He takes it with him everywhere. If I were to speak to you about the duties of citizenship you would perhaps ask me "Where is my country?" and think you had confounded me. You would be wrong, however. You must not say: "What does it matter to me where I live?" It does matter that you should be where you can fulfil all your duties as a man, and one of these duties is to be loyal to the place of your birth. Your fellow-countrymen protected you in childhood. They are entitled to your love when you become a man. You should live among them, or wherever you can be most useful to them. For that, I am not urging you to go and reside in a big town. On the contrary, one of the examples good men can give to others is that of a patriarchal life in the country. That was the first life of man, and still the finest and most natural to those with unspoiled hearts.' I like to think how Emile and Sophie in their simple retreat may spread benefits around them, putting fresh life into the country and reviving the worn-out spirits of unfortunate villagers.

THE MARRIAGE OF EMILE AND SOPHIE

At last I see approaching the most delightful day in Emile's life and the happiest in mine. I see the crown set on my labours. The goodly couple are united in an indissoluble bond. Their lips utter and their hearts confirm enduring vows. They are wedded.

'My children,' I say to them as I take them both by the hand, 'it is three years since I saw the beginnings of the ardent love that makes you happy today. It has gone on growing steadily, and I see from your eyes that now it has reached its greatest intensity. After this it can only decline.' My readers can imagine the indignant vows of Emile, and the scornful air with which Sophie withdraws her hand from mine, and the protesting glances of mutual adoration they exchange. I let them have their way, and then I proceed. 'I have often thought that if it were possible to prolong the happiness of love in marriage we would have a heaven on earth. Would you like me to tell you what in my belief is the only way to secure that?' They look at each other with a mocking smile. 'It is simple and easy,' I continue. 'It is to go on being lovers after you are married.' 'That will not be hard for us,' says Emile, laughing at my secret. 'Perhaps harder than you think,' I reply. 'Knots which are too tightly drawn break. That is what happens to the marriage tie when too great a strain is put on it. The faithfulness required of a married couple is the most sacred of all obligations but the power it gives one partner over the other is too great. Constraint and love go ill together, and the pleasures of marriage are not to be had on demand, It is impossible to make a duty of tender affection and to treat the sweetest pledges of love as a right. What right there is comes from mutual desire: nature knows no other. Neither belongs to the other except by his or her own good will. Both must remain master of their persons and their caresses.

'When Emile became your husband, Sophie, he became your head and by the will of nature you owe him obedience. But when the wife is like you it is good for the husband to be guided by her: that is also the law of nature and it gives you as much authority over his heart as his sex gives him over your person. Make yourself dear to him by your favours and respected by your refusals. On these terms you will get his confidence; he will listen to your advice and settle nothing without consulting you. After love has lasted a considerable time a sweet habit takes its place, and the attraction of confidence succeeds the transports of passion. When you cease to be Emile's mistress you will be his wife and sweetheart and the mother of his children, and you will enjoy the closest intimacy. Remember that if your husband lives happily with you, you will be a happy woman.'

'Dear Emile,' I say to the young husband, 'all through life a man has need of a counsellor and guide. Up to the present I have tried to fulfil that duty to you. At this point my lengthy task comes to an end and another takes it over. Today I abdicate the authority you have allowed me. From this time on, Sophie is your tutor.'

Gradually the first rapture calms down and leaves them to experience in peace the delights of their new state. Happy lovers, worthy spouses! How often I am enraptured as I contemplate my work in them, and my heart beats quicker. How often I take their hands in mine, blessing Providence and uttering heartfelt sighs; and they in their turn are affected and share my transports. If happiness is to be found anywhere in earth, it is to be found in the retreat where we live.

Some months later Emile comes into my room and embraces me. 'Master,' he says, 'congratulate your boy. He hopes soon to have the honour to be a father. There will be new cares for us and for you. I do not mean to let you bring up the son as you have brought up the father. God forbid that a task so sweet and holy should fall to any one but me. But remain the teacher of the young teachers. Advise and direct us, and we will be ready to learn. I will have need of you as long as I live. I need you more than ever now that the tasks of my manhood are beginning. You have completed your own tasks. Lead me to imitate you, and enjoy your well-earned rest.

EDITOR'S EPILOGUE

Natural Education

Having followed Emile in his educational career from birth to marriage, we have now to look back and ask what there was in this romantic tale to impress so many of Rousseau's contemporaries and give a new direction to education up to our own time. The question is easier to answer for the eighteenth century than for the twentieth. At the time of its composition, Rousseau was living insecurely among people of wealth and rank, whose families were all being educated tutorially at home. The book in its present form was intended for the edification and entertainment of some of his patronesses, for whom he turned what was originally meant to be a treatise into a kind of a story that would serve to enlighten them about the education of their families. The general scheme was certainly different from the ordinary practice in some respects, but not nearly so different as it is from ours. The story form of the exposition, it is true, presented some difficulty. Did Rousseau mean the story to be taken literally? Did he think that boys and girls should be, or could be, educated like Emile and Sophie? When asked, Rousseau sometimes said 'Yes' and sometimes said 'No.' Actually there was no reason for not saying 'Yes.' The tutor acting *in loco parentis* and demanding complete authority made an obvious difficulty. But as Rousseau himself made clear at the beginning and again at the end of the book, the tutor was incidental to the story and not essential to it. The real educators in a 'natural' education, he was careful to insist, were the father and mother. In the good family, there is just such a control of conditions and just such individual guidance to the child as the symbolical tutor provides in the *Emile*. That indeed is how Rousseau depicts the ideal education in the *Nouvelle Heloïse*.

It was true for his first readers: it continues true for us. The family plays a fundamental part in the right ordering of every child's life. That, as Rousseau would say, is in accordance with nature.

A further qualification is needed. The suggestion given in the opening sections of the *Emile* is that as things are the individualised education here set forth is the only natural education. If society is unnatural, he tells us, we must choose between making a man and making a citizen: we cannot make both. There are, he says, two kinds of education, communal (or public) education, individual (or domestic) education: in seeming opposition, but not really opposed. Emile in France gets the individual training to make the best of his native powers, because citizenship in great nation states like France and England (according to Rousseau) involves the sacrifice of the natural individuality, which is everyone's birthright. If Emile had been born in Geneva, or in a city state like Plato's *Republic*, or if the modern state could be reformed so that its citizens could preserve their original nature, it would be different. Education would then make both man and citizen. Actually Rousseau himself managed to effect some kind of reconciliation in the *Emile*. Emile, after being protected from socialisation in his childhood, ends up as a country gentleman in full membership of the community he serves. And eleven years after writing the *Emile* Rousseau went over to the advocacy of national education in *Considerations on the Government of Poland*, in which he prescribes the fashioning of the minds of young Poles as the only sure way of saving Poland. He does not stop to think about the 'saving' of the young Poles. Doubtless he would have argued, as Plato argued, as indeed he himself argued in regard to the young Genevese, that in good citizenship they would find full personal satisfaction. But whatever the argument, the fact remains that there is always bound to be some loss of individuality in the process by which the child becomes man through a social upbringing. That is why the *Emile*, one-sided as it is, continues to be worthy of study in the twentieth century. In spite of the broadening freedoms of the democratic nations and their recognition of the necessity for respecting the personal lives of their peoples, there is still a real danger in an era of great industrial populations, mass production, universal conscription, broadcasting, compulsory education, that the spirit of man may be overwhelmed by the community. That has happened disastrously in the dictator countries in the present century. Unless there be deliberate precaution in our own education, in home and in school, it may happen to us.

What then is the enduring lesson of the *Emile*? Not that every child needs a teacher all to himself to organise his social environment and to direct and guide him in his upgrowing. The child does need the right environment and does need guidance. But between the family and the various social agencies (notably the school) there is a reasonable chance that the ordinary child will not fare too badly as he moves forward to his maturity as man and citizen. There may even be virtue in the need for some adaptation on his own part where his elders fail him. The tutor and the tutorial education under country conditions had their place in the aristocratic way of life in the eighteenth century, but they are merely incidents in Rousseau's discussion of education. The big truth in his view, the truth that gives it application to the education of the children of all times and all conditions, is that the educator should take full account of human nature, and especially the nature of the child. Begin by studying the child, he said; and by not merely saying it, but by trying to do it himself in this book about Emile, he impressed the idea on all subsequent education.

The task he set himself and us was not an easy one. There is a seeming simplicity about the idea of making education conform to nature. It can be translated into everyday language as a call to use common sense and see the foolishness of social usages which have lost their meaning and possibly have even become harmful. The insistence by Rousseau on sensible methods of feeding and clothing babies, and again on the learning of some trade in the teens as an insurance against an uncertain future, illustrates its value. But get deeper down into the maxim, and philosophical and scientific problems, not to mention problems of practice, make their appearance. Leaving aside the question of what 'nature' is, we may ask what is 'human nature?' What again is implied in speaking of the 'nature' of the child? Rousseau has his own answers to these questions, and he gives them in a way that challenges us to agreement or disagreement.

In the forefront of his theory of life is his conviction that man in himself, man as a natural being, is good. Here he breaks with the Calvinism of Geneva: according to him if man in society is bad, it is not because he is bad by nature but because he has been made bad by society. Actually the goodness with which he credits man is of a rather neutral kind. It is not that child or man can be allowed to do what he likes and that he will inevitably take the right course, but rather that if he is not led into vice or error by others he will come to make the right adaptation to the necessities of the natural and the social worlds, and so reach truth and virtue. The way of the good life is a hard way: happiness can only be achieved by keeping desire within the limits imposed by the nature of things. The educational implication of this doctrine for Rosseau are interesting. The postulate of the scheme is that in man there is an active principle at work. The child does not become good or intelligent by having the habits or the opinions of society imposed on him. What he does or knows should be the outcome of a personal reaction on life situations. The truth for me is what I have convinced myself is true: the good I appreciate by the inner light. The difficulty is that such response as a child can make to life is limited to sense-given facts. The ordinary instruction supplies him with ready-made habits and views ahead of the time when he can understand things and form his own judgments. That in Rousseau's opinion is what makes it bad. What is learned at second-hand in this way prevents him learning things for himself when he attains the necessary maturity.

Better therefore no education than one that prejudices the future development like this. There is plenty of time for morals and science when the mind is able to do its proper work. Indoctrination is always wrong.

The realisation of the difference between child and man is fundamental in the new education Rousseau advocated. To take proper account of the child's nature at its different stages, it is necessary to make such a study of childhood as no one had even attempted before his time. What are the essential differences between a child of 2 and a child of 10? Between a child of 10, and one of 16 or 18 or 20? These are hard questions to answer, and it cannot be said that Rousseau or any of his successors has been altogether successful in answering them. But in trying to define the mental changes which take place as the child grows by successive changes into manhood he made some important advances towards a dynamic psychology. He still talked as if the mind were made up of a number of separate faculties, which appear one after another: sensations in infancy, sense judgments in childhood, practical thinking in the early teens, reasoning and abstraction in adolescence. But in contrast with the materialistic philosophers with whom he shared this faculty psychology, he recognised the existence of a co-ordinating self that is active at all stages of life. While he emphasised the fact that it was the child's right to live a full life as a child and professed himself indifferent to his future occupation, he knew quite well that the child needs the right kind of training for manhood. Thinking in terms of mental self-activity, he anticipated later psychology by connecting physical and mental energy. It is the powers set free by the growth of the body in the early teens that extend the child's intellectual horizon. Even more important, it is the physical changes of puberty that bring about the manifold transformations of adolescence. Rousseau's discussion of adolescence from this point of view was a revolutionary event in educational thought.

It is easy to criticise much of what Rousseau wrote about the education of the child at the different periods of immature life. It is evident to us now that in stressing the differences between one period and another he did less than justice to the continuity of growth; that in fact he met the one-sidedness of common practice which ignores these differences with a one-sidedness of his own. Children are adults in the making: children have their rights as children and their own way of life. There is truth in both views. But as happens with adults, always more concerned about their own side of the relation with children, the half-truth most needing attention is the one with which Rousseau challenged his own age and still challenges ours. The new education he initiated attempts to secure a proper balance by trying to take into account the distinctive nature of the child in the education that fits him for society. Its aim is to make both man and citizen, but it gives special thought to the making of the man.

The problem of effecting a reconciliation of the interests of society and the individual with which Rousseau wrestles in the *Emile* is still with us. It is in fact the problem of democracy, and of the schooling which prepares boys and girls for the democratic way of life; and we all of us are democratic enough to take it for granted that home and school and the adult communities to which we belong should bring personal satisfaction through our membership of them. The problem has been largely solved in the good home, and we are trying to solve it in the good school. What help has Rousseau to give us here? Does his discussion of curriculum and methods in the *Emile*, when taken out of its story setting, have any useful applications in the work of the modern school?

Let us begin with his scheme for education in boyhood in Book Two. The emphasis here is largely on what he calls 'negative education'—on the habits and ideas the boy is not to acquire. There are really two different lines of thought in this, and it is important to distinguish them. The one is that it only does harm to children to teach them things that are beyond personal comprehension and appreciation. If history or literature or morals or religion need a mature mind to have significance—as Rousseau firmly believes—they can only be taught verbally in childhood, and the verbal learning will prejudice the deeper experiences of later life. The other line is that even if it is possible to teach children to read or write or count, it is a mistake to do so before they are conscious of the need for them. The only satisfactory motive for learning is the interest on the level of childhood that comes from realised need. With the latter, intelligent teachers are in the main agreed: the practical difficulty experienced in putting the idea into practice is met (up to a point) by some form of the project method, in which the learner is set to a task of his own choosing which makes it necessary for him to read, write or count. The former raises more serious issues, because it runs counter to the universal practice of indoctrinating children with the great social ideals and faiths. Children, we say, must learn to be good. They must have impressed on them the best things in our social heritage; science, art, literature, music. They must be brought up in the religious faith of their fathers. But what if the children are not really learning the lessons we think we are teaching them? Take history, for example: what can immature persons of limited knowledge, and possibly of limited intelligence, make of the complex sequences and interrelations of events that constitute any great social movement, or of the personalities of those taking part in them? Or again think of religion with its combination of dogma and worship; what personal meaning can it have for children before the awakening of mind and spirit at adolescence? In the whole cultural domain, there is good cause for paying heed to Rousseau's warning against premature instruction. With his usual vehemence of conviction he has over-stated his case. Every adult capacity has its origins in childhood. Some sense of beauty, some realisation of the past, some religious awe, some of the wonder out of which science comes are present from the earliest years. The spiritual faculties must all be nurtured by the appropriate culture from the beginning of life. But so long as adults think of children as but smaller editions of themselves, and fail to realise their mental and moral limitations, Rousseau's emphasis on what children cannot learn, and should not learn, will serve to remind parents and teachers that children must be allowed to act and think as persons in their own right, if they are ever to achieve full personality. In school practice there is no need for the clean sweep of adult interests which Rousseau seems to advocate in the case of Emile. He himself shows the way to a sane child-centred education in the case of mathematics. In effect, his method was to make the pupil want to learn, and thereafter teach him by an appeal to concrete experiences in his everyday life. The same course can be taken within the limits of childish capacity in every sphere. Partly by looking on at grown-up ways, partly by enjoying the simpler unintellectualised experiences in the aesthetic, moral and religious spheres, the child gets prepared for his future life without knowing it. In the light of all the educational experiments made since Rousseau's time in his spirit, it is possible to conceive of a school in which children sharing in community life may get a real initiation into the varied richness of humanity, without losing the satisfactions of a happy childhood.

The educational scheme for the teen-ages before and after puberty, set forth in Books Three and Four, presents fewer difficulties to the modern reader of Rousseau than the scheme for boyhood. Allowing for the differences between the eighteenth and the twentieth centuries, he will find himself in considerable agreement with much that is said about the teaching of science and of the humanities. Even if critical of the view that social understanding does not come till after puberty, and that consequently the social studies cannot be included between 12 and 15, he will accept Rousseau's admission of geography and physical science at this stage as in accord with present experience and practice, and will appreciate the value assigned to craftsmanship both for the immediate interest and as a preparation for the future. The organisation of adolescent education round the developing sex interest, again, gives a view of what is happening as the young man or woman moves onward through personal friendships and the broad human relations to life as a member of society, which was quite new when first propounded, and which has not lost its freshness even yet. Just as the primary school is inclined to stress instrumental arts like reading, writing and counting, with more concern about their later use than their present interest, so the secondary school stresses the more complex instruments of languages, mathematics, sciences and arts for their utility in the occupations and pursuits that lie ahead. Rousseau's lively account of the personal training in history, language, economics, religion and literature in response to the needs of youth serves as a reminder that the making of the worthy man is quite as important as the making of the good citizen; and that in order to achieve this the adolescent studies must not only prepare for the future but yield their own proper satisfactions in their season.

Finally come, in Book Five, the education of Sophie and the last stages of Emile's education. The education of men and women, he maintains, must be fundamentally different. By reason of their sex they differ in character and temperament: man strong and active, woman weak and passive; man dominating woman, woman holding her own by the charms that make her pleasing to man. Their natures being different they must be educated differently: the boy to be independent of public opinion and recognising no authority but what approves itself to him, the girl to be socially docile, accepting the authority of parents in childhood and later of husband and society. Here plainly 'Nature' speaks the language of eighteenth century prejudice. Even so it would be a mistake to dismiss Rousseau's views too lightly. Under the conditions of the modern democratic community we have discovered that women are in no way inferior to men in intellectual ability or practical aptitude; and there is reason to believe that some at least of the mental and moral differences of the sexes are due to social training. It still remains true that masculinity and femininity are mutually enriching as complements in the family life and in the wider interests of the community. It is possible that our mass systems of schooling, standardised by examination tests and national requirements, may have ironed out differences between the sexes in the field of education, to the detriment of the persons concerned and of society as a whole. We do not yet know how deep sex differences go in human personality. There is need for longer experience and further investigation. Rousseau may be right in thinking that there should be a very considerable difference in the two educations—and we may be wrong in minimising it.

In any case, the value of Rousseau's discussion of the age and sex differences in education depends not on his practical suggestions but on the basic principles which have found expression in his educational writings. He himself says as much in the preface to the *Emile*, and his followers, through whom his teaching has passed into the stream of European thought, have confirmed it by developing methods of their own very different from his. The question for us is not whether we should educate children in Rousseau's way but whether there is essential truth in the idea of a 'natural' education as propounded by him. The assumption that underlies the view of education presented in the *Emile* is that children are living, growing beings who at every stage of their upgrowing are persons in their own right, capable of being properly prepared for later maturity only through the active interests of their own age and condition. It is in effect the democratic conception of humanity applied to childhood and youth, and is accepted in some fashion by all modern educators as an integral element in the educational ideal. Even if in their practice they find it an ideal hard to realise and are sometimes faithless to its spirit, the schools of today (we hope) are moving slowly but surely towards an education that will make their pupils both citizens and men: a national and a natural education.

There still remains the question with which we began the study of the *Emile*. How did Rousseau come to write this unique book which has given modern education a fresh orientation in the direction of democracy and set all sorts of people on the quest for new ways of schooling with a regard for the individual child? His first approaches to the practical problem were certainly not very promising. He had achieved literary reputation unexpectedly by a somewhat perverse *Discourse on the Sciences and the Arts*, written for a prize offered by the Academy of Dijon. The story goes that when he was pondering how to deal with the subject, he met Diderot, and on his advice decided to make an attack on all forms of learning as sources of social corruption and depravity. 'The affirmative view,' said Diderot, 'is the bridge for the asses. All the mediocrities will take that road and only find commonplace ideas on it; whereas the opposite view opens up a rich field for philosophy and eloquence.' Rousseau took the advice because it suited his own anti-social mentality, and proceeded to pile up arguments to prove the badness of civilisation and the learning on which it is based. His views on education—but one item in a mass of confused exposition—anticipate the views he developed later in the *Emile*, and reveal the state of mind in which they had their origin. 'If the cultivation of the sciences is prejudicial to the martial qualities of a people,' he wrote, 'it is even more so to their morals. From the first years an absurd education clutters up our minds and distorts our judgment. On all hands are to be seen great institutions where young people are taught everything but their duty. They are ignorant of their mother tongue and yet learn other languages that are of no use anywhere. They can compose verses which are almost beyond their own comprehension. They cannot distinguish truth from error, but they have the art of confusing others by specious arguments. With all this, they do not know what words like "magnanimity," "equity," "temperance," "humanity" and "courage" mean. The goodly word "fatherland" never is heard by them and if they hear mention of God, it is as a being to be dreaded rather than revered. What then should they learn? A fine question that. Let them learn what they will need to do when they come to be men and not things they had better forget.' The spirit of this first *Discourse* was still active when he came to write the

Emile. Do the opposite of what is usually done, he could tell his readers, and you will be right. This is dangerous talk. It could easily lead a man into futile eccentricity, or even in the extreme case into madness. Rousseau himself did not wholly escape this penalty. On the other hand, it makes possible to the saint or the man of genius moral and intellectual insights denied to men of more conventional minds. These exceptional persons rebel against the accepted convictions and customs on which the lives of ordinary men and women are based, and sometimes, when by a happy chance they combine constructive power with the refusal to follow the common ways, they open up new vistas for mankind. Rousseau was one of these. His mind was original in amazing degree and he pioneered in many directions, notably in politics and in education.

The revolutionary idea in education, expressed with strange compelling power in the *Emile*, is at once simple and profound. It is, in a word, that education to be effective in the making of good human beings and through them of a good society, must be child-centred. Educators before him had stressed the need to take proper account of the child's point of view, but always they had thought of children as limited creatures requiring to be fashioned after the adult pattern. Jesus indeed had set the child in the midst and told the older people that they must become as children if they were to enter the kingdom of heaven, but till Rousseau nobody had ever tried to give practical effect to this precept. It was because poor frustrated Rousseau had so much of the child in himself that he was able to look at life through the eyes of a child, and appreciate the child's point of view. And thus he was led to realise, as no one had done before, that it was only by living his own kind of life in all its fullness that the child could develop into adult man. From that conception of the child as a being with rights and duties on his own level of experience everything else followed: the idea of natural education (that is, of education in accordance with the nature of the child); the need for definite knowledge of children, both boys and girls, at the successive stages of their growth, and the need also for a knowledge of their individual characteristics; the training for life through life in a country environment from which all influences that might lead to vice or error are excluded by a wise direction; the limitation of learning to matters of personal concern and interest till maturity brings fitness for adult studies; the impersonal discipline of consequences to check waywardness and misconduct. These principles, presented concretely in the romantic tale of Emile and Sophie, and interwoven in more abstract form with the biographical detail, laid hold on the imagination of a great number of Rousseau's contemporaries. Fathers and mothers paid him the compliment of believing that their children should be educated like the original pair. Educators in various lands—outstanding men like Kant and Pestalozzi—were led to re-think their opinions about education and to devise ways and means of creating a better education suited to their own conditions. The French Revolution and its aftermath brought a reaction, and Rousseau and his works sank for a time in common esteem, but the magic of the *Emile* never wholly lost its power and its essential ideas gradually found their way into the educational ideals, and to some extent into the educational practice, of Europe. These ideas were in the main the inspiring faith of the New Schools which came into being in England, America, Germany and other countries at the end of the nineteenth and the beginning of the twentieth century, and they have since spread over the world through the New Education Fellowship.

National Education

Most people think of Rousseau as the apostle of individualism in education. The reason for that is not hard to find. The lack of a fatherland to inspire devotion and give a big purpose to life, which Rousseau notes again and again as characteristic of the modern world with its great nation states, compels thinking men to seek an inner sufficiency. Rousseau, a Swiss living a lonely, alien life in France, could not well be anything but an individualist. The *Emile* in which a grown-up Rousseau educates a Rousseau child was inevitably individualistic in its outlook, and the fact that the story was about the upbringing of one particular boy emphasised the one-sidedness. It is little wonder that most people, knowing Rousseau's views on education through the *Emile*, think that that is all there is to them.

Actually there is another view never very far from Rousseau's thought. The reader of the *Emile* gets a glimpse of it when Rousseau has occasion to refer to Plato and his ideal state with its wise philosopher kings. Plato belonged to the Golden Age to which Rousseau had been introduced in his boyhood in the pages of Plutarch. 'Constantly occupied with Rome and Athens, living as it were with their great men, myself born the citizen of a republic, the son of a father whose ruling passion was the love of his country, I was set on fire by his example.' Here in the ancient world he had found a fatherland of the spirit, to which he went back in any discussion of community life and government. There was added significance for him in the doings of the old-time city states in the fact that he had grown up in a modern city state himself. He had all the passionate pride of the exile in his own Geneva. Everywhere else social relations might be wrongly ordered, virtue might be denied its due reward and vice escape merited punishment. Geneva was the one happy exception. 'Having had the good fortune to be born among you,' he wrote in the dedication of the *Discourse on Inequality* to the Republic of Geneva, 'I could not but meditate on the equality nature had conferred on men and the inequality they had created for themselves, without thinking of the profound wisdom with which the two had been happily combined in this state. In my search for the best principles which good sense might prescribe for the constitution of a government I have been so much impressed at finding them all in operation in yours, that even if I had not been born within your walls I would have felt myself obliged to depict

Geneva as the human society outstripping that of all peoples in its advantages.' There is extravagance in this, perhaps permissible in a dedication, but it does express Rousseau's sincere conviction about the fundamental rightness of life in the city of his birth. His whole social philosophy drew largely on this glorified Geneva. It was the ground of the faith which gave definiteness and reality to his political ideas and saved him from cynicism.

From the memories of his childhood and youth and his studies of classical institutions came the idea of an acceptable national education, complementary to the tutorial system idealised in the *Emile*: two streams of thought which so far as Rousseau was concerned never came together. When he was discussing education with his patronesses or planning for the upbringing of Emile, private education was his theme: when speculating about government, it was public education in the interests of the community as a whole. In the latter case education is not treated by him as a separate issue but only in the context of some form of social organisation. There are three such discussions: two nearly contemporaneous with the writing of the *Emile*—in an article on Political Economy written for the *Encyclopédie* and in the defence of Genevan institutions in his *Letter to M. d'Alembert*; the third written eleven years after the publication of *Emile*, among his *Considerations for the Government of Poland*.

Political Economy: The subject of national education makes its first appearance in the *Encyclopédie* article on what is designated political economy, but which should more properly have been called Politics, the Principles of Government. The article is not very good. It is flat, diffuse, over general, lacking the animation and the circumstantial detail which give Rousseau's major writings their inspiring power. One almost gets the impression that he had not yet got his mind clear about the general implications of government and was writing against the grain. Nevertheless the article is important for the understanding of Rousseau, because it shows his thought in the making. The essentials of the problem of combining personal freedom with government are all there even if still rather vague. There is a suggestion of an idealistic conception of the state in his mention of it as 'the Whole,' a unifying entity and not a mere aggregation of individuals, and in the postulate of a 'General Will.' The concept of the General Will, which was to become of the greatest significance in his later political thinking, makes its first appearance here and from it Rousseau comes to the idea of national education as necessary to bring the general will of the community and the particular wills of the citizens into working concord.

Here is the gist of the article in Rousseau's own words:

'A real nation cannot exist without freedom any more than freedom can exist without virtue. Make the citizen good by proper training and everything else follows. Without that there will only be a nation of slaves, including the rulers. Such a civic education is not the affair of a day. If from infancy children are led to think of their personal interests as completely bound up with the interests of the state and never to regard their own existence as having any meaning apart from it, they will come in time to identify themselves in some measure with the grand Whole and become conscious of themselves as members of their country. It is too late to change the natural dispositions once they have taken their own course and have been strengthened by habit. A heart occupied by avarice, lust and vanity has no room in it for one's fellow citizens.

'It cannot be left to the individual man to be sole judge as to his duties. Still less should children's education be left to the ignorance and prejudice of their fathers. The matter is of far greater concern to the state than to the fathers. The state abides, the family passes. In any case, if the government takes the place of the fathers by undertaking this important function the fathers have little cause to complain. All that is involved is a change of name. They will exercise in common as citizens the same rights as they exercised separately as fathers, and get as ready obedience when they speak in the name of the law as they did when they spoke in the name of nature. Public education, regulated by the state, under magistrates appointed by the supreme authority, is an essential condition of popular government. If children are educated together as equals and have the laws of the state and the maxims of the general will instilled into them as worthy of respect above all else, they will assuredly learn to regard each other as brothers, and to desire only what the community desires. In course of time they themselves will become the defenders and fathers of the country whose children they have been.'

The scheme is left vague except in regard to the men who are to administer it. Here Rousseau borrows from Plato the idea of entrusting guardianship to men of standing who have proved themselves by their previous conduct in the service of the state. 'The magistrates to whom it falls to superintend this education,' he says, 'must be men who have discharged worthily every other office of state.' But he goes beyond Plato (and sense) in making the magistrates themselves the teachers. 'Let famous soldiers preach courage and upright judges teach justice. Such teachers will create virtuous successors and enable the experience and talents of the rulers and the virtues of the citizens to be passed on from generation to generation.'

Geneva's Public Education: Seemingly Rousseau had forgotten his own Geneva when he wrote the *Encyclopédie* article. More likely, the difference of the lives of his fellow citizens from anything in the ancient city states caused him to miss the fact that Geneva had its own kind of 'public' education. The discovery came to him in the course of writing a very lengthy *Letter to M. d'Alembert*, the distinguished French scholar, protesting against the suggestion made in his article on Geneva in the seventh volume of the *Encyclopédie*, that a theatre for the playing of French comedies should be established in Geneva. Rousseau saw in the plays and in the comedians who would present them a threat to all that was best in the traditions of his people. D'Alembert had said that the theatrical performances would help to form the taste

of the citizens and give them a sensitive judgment and a
delicacy of sentiment difficult to acquire otherwise. Rousseau
with Calvinistic distrust of the theatre was convinced, on the
other hand, that they would speedily corrupt both taste and
morals. In the course of a varied argument that ranges widely
over questions of literature and conduct there emerged in
his *Letter* a wonderfully complete picture of the culture
manifest in the everyday life of the little Swiss city.

Life in Geneva, as he pointed out, is very different from
what it is in a great capital city like Paris. In a small town
there is less excitement and less rush, and the needs of life
make fewer demands on the inhabitants. The greater leisure
allows time for thought, and consequently there is more
originality and invention and a greater chance of new things
happening. Even more important was the background of
industry and commerce which gave the city its bourgeois
character. There were a few very wealthy people and a few
living in poverty, but the great majority were well-to-do
people living in the easy comfort ensured by hard work,
thrift and moderation. The stranger coming into Geneva
could not but be struck by the prevailing vigour: everybody
busy, everybody moving about, everybody fully occupied with
work and business. In one quarter he would find a greater
assembly of watch- and clock-making than anywhere else in
Europe: in another, all the activities of a world-wide commerce, suggesting a sea port rather than an inland town; in
still another, several noisy factories engaged in the production
of printed calicoes. No need here for the entertainments of
an idle people.

This varied work carried on in an atmosphere of freedom,
he points out, had made a deep impression on the character
of the citizens. Even the artisans (according to Rousseau)
were superior to those of any other country. A watchmaker
of Geneva, he told a correspondent who had criticised his
Letter to d'Alembert, could hold his own in any society,
whereas a Parisian workman could talk only of watches.
Rousseau himself had been brought up among the *horlogers*—

his father had been a watchmaker at one time—and he instanced a remarkable community engaged in the craft in a mountain village near Neufchâtel, in proof of his contention. It was not only that these peasants were good watchmakers, but that they spent their leisure in the making of a thousand articles by hand. 'In the winter-time especially, when the depth of the snow makes outside communication difficult, each of them shuts himself up warmly with his numerous family in the good wooden house of his own construction, and busies himself with a multitude of entertaining tasks which drive dull care away and add to his well-being. Every man is his own joiner, locksmith, glazier or turner, and all the articles of furniture in the house have been made by the master. And in addition they have time enough to invent and make a thousand different instruments of steel, wood or cardboard for sale to strangers. They even make watches, each man almost unbelievably combining in himself all the different branches of the watch- and clock-making trade. But that is not all. They have technical books and are tolerably well educated. They can all sketch, paint and cypher a little. Most of them play the flute, and quite a number have a little music and can sing in tune. One of their common pleasures is to sing the psalms in four parts with their wives and children. These many arts have not been taught them by masters but have come to them through the village tradition.' (One recalls here the virtue imputed to village life in the early education of Emile.)

No less important for the making of good men and good citizens, Rousseau insists, were the leisure-time occupations of the people of Geneva. They were an open-air people, fond of wandering over the country side, of hunting, of boating on the Lake; and the military exercises carried through by the civic army every spring created bonds of friendship among the men. This had led to the formation of a large number of what they called 'circles' or clubs, consisting of groups of from a dozen to fifteen men. These clubs usually met in a tavern, and there in the afternoon associates in business or pleasure foregathered to pursue the amusements of their taste—playing, talking, reading, drinking, smoking. The women and girls for their part had their own groups, meeting in each other's houses for a game of cards, a bite of food and endless chatter. Such were their daily amusements: simple and innocent as befitted the republican morals.

The other side of their social training came through their common interests. The objection made to Comedy by those like Rousseau on grounds of taste and morals did not mean that spectacles had no place in a republic like Geneva. What people, he asked, have better reason for coming together often for joyful assembly? Actually there was already in the city quite a number of regular gatherings on public occasions. Every year there were military reviews, presentations of prizes, elections of kings of the arquebus, of the cannon, of navigation. There was no reason, he said, why such festivals should not be multiplied. Workmen are as important for the republic as soldiers. Why not found prizes for wrestling, running, throwing the discus and other physical exercise on the model of the military awards? Why not encourage the boatmen by having contests on the Lake? Only those who have taken an active part in the existing festivals can appreciate the ardour with which the people of Geneva enter into them. They are no longer recognisable as the subdued people who refuse to depart from their economic rules, or the rational beings who weigh everything, including their jokes, in the balance of judgment. On such occasions all are lively and gay, and ready to share their happiness with their fellows. The various social groups come together freely. It is almost a matter of indifference at which table they sit down. Everywhere there is a sense of community.

When making this analysis of the formative influences which gave the people of Geneva their distinctive character, Rousseau seems scarcely aware of the educational implications of his argument. It was not till he received a letter from a Dr. Tronchin, condemning clubs and all forms of public amusement as time-wasting and prejudicial to family life and domestic education, that he realised that what he had been expounding was a modern form of public education comparable with that of the ancient states whose practices he admired and quoted. It was as the son of an artisan, born and brought up in Geneva, he said in his reply, that he himself had 'received this public education, not from any specific instruction, but from those traditions and precepts which are passed on from one generation to another and impress on young people at an early age the knowledge and sentiments they ought to acquire.' It was not true that children who had been educated in this informal way were left to grow up any way at all. The teachings of the home came in to supplement their social training. 'It is in the home,' he adds, 'that children should be educated, the girls by the mother and the boys by the father. This is the right education for the people of Geneva, midway between the public education of the Greek republics and the isolating domestic education of the present-day monarchies.' (But in all this there is not a word about Geneva's Academy.)

A New Education for Poland: In the closing years of Rousseau's life, when his creative energies had got bogged in the recording of unhappy memories, there came by a happy chance a request for guidance from a Polish patriot, which led him to put his ideas about national education into definite form. The appeal was made to the author of the *Social Contract*, but so far as education was concerned it was the author of the *Emile*, seeking to apply the principles of individual education to the individual nation, who made reply. What was wanted was a scheme for the reform of the Polish government which would give Poland internal stability and enable her to withstand Russian aggression. That, Rousseau was quick to realise, was as much a matter of education as of politics. It pleased him to think of himself as performing a task similar to the law-makers of the ancient world—Moses, Lycurgus and Numa Pompilius. 'The same spirit guided these ancient legislators in their institutions,' he said. 'They sought for ties to bind the citizens to their country and to their fellows, and they found them in distinctive national usages: in exclusive religious ceremonies, in games that gave sense of community, in physical exercises which increased vigour and strength as well as pride and self esteem, in historical spectacles which recalled their ancestors and quickened them to a lively emulation and kept the fatherland always in their thoughts.'

The greater part of the *Memorandum on the Government of Poland* is devoted to questions of constitution and administration, but Rousseau was well aware that what the Poles needed even more than political reform was a change of heart. That was why he put education in the forefront of his scheme. The only way to get to the hearts of the people, he said, was through education; but it must be the right kind of education, not the education of the ordinary teachers who think only of force and punishments and rely on material rewards, but one that stirs the heart and creates a love for the country and its laws. How was this to be effected? 'Dare I say it? Through children's games and institutions commonly regarded as of no account on a superficial view which nevertheless form precious habits and unbreakable attachments.'

The immediate problem for the Poles was to save themselves from being swallowed up by their powerful neighbours, and losing their identity as a nation. There was only one way, according to Rousseau, by which this could be prevented. The Poles must resist the tendency to uniformity which made Frenchmen, Germans, Spaniards, and even Englishmen, Europeans and nothing besides. 'Make it impossible for a Pole ever to become a Russian, and I can guarantee that Russia will never conquer Poland.' His advice was that they should preserve, and if need be restore, their national traditions. They were fortunate in having a garb of their own. If their king and their public men were always to wear this the time would come when no Pole would ever appear in court in French apparel. Another good thing from this point of view was public games: not the ordinary amusements of courts which made men effeminate and led them to forget their own country but, if necessary, new games, festivals and ceremonies, Polish in spirit.

There should also be open-air spectacles, not confined to the rich and the great, in which everybody could share. The circuses in which young Poles had taken an active part until quite recent times should be re-established to serve as theatres of honour and emulation. It would be easy to substitute for the cruel combats which once took place in them, physical exercises calling for strength and skill, in which the victors would receive due honours and rewards. Horsemanship, for example, was an activity well fitted for Poles, which would lend itself readily to spectacular display.

From national institutions, Rousseau passes to national education. This, he says, as he begins the discussion of Education (Chap. IV), is the article that matters most.

'It is education that should put the national stamp on men's minds and give the direction to their opinions and tastes which will make them patriots. From birth and all through life the child should only have eyes for his native country. It is love of country that makes a man what he is. By himself he counts for nothing. If he loses his fatherland, life ends so far as he is concerned: if not dead, he is worse than dead. National education is the privilege of free men who share common interests and are united under law. Young Frenchmen, Englishmen, Spaniards, Italians, Russians are all much the same when they leave college. A Pole at twenty should be different: he should be nothing but a Pole. When he is learning to read I would have him read about his own country. At ten he should be acquainted with all its products: at twelve with all its provinces, roadways and towns. At fifteen he should know all its history: at sixteen all its laws. There should not be a noble deed or distinguished man in all Poland but are so enshrined in heart and memory that he can give instant account of them. From this it will be evident that it is not the ordinary kind of instruction imparted by foreigners and priests that I have in mind for children. The subject matter, sequence and character of their studies should be regulated by law. Their teachers should be Poles, preferably married men, destined after a period of years for other occupations, not more important or more honourable, but less exacting and more distinguished. In any case, teaching must not be allowed to become a profession. No public man in Poland should hold any permanent post but that of citizen. Every post a man occupies, and particularly important ones like teaching, should be regarded simply as a test of competence, a stage by which he can mount still higher according to his deserts.

'I dislike the distinction between colleges and academies which leads the rich nobles and the poor nobles to get a different education. Since from the constitutional point of view they are equals, they should be educated together and get the same education. Even if it is not possible to have a completely free system of public education, the fees should be made so low that even the poorest can pay them. There might even be made available in all the colleges a number of free places at the expense of the state. If these places were granted to the children of poor gentle-folk, not as a charity but as a reward for good services done by their fathers, they would become a mark of distinction and serve a double purpose. Those who secured the nomination might be called the children of the state and given precedence over other children of their age.

'In all the colleges a gymnasium for physical exercises should be established. This much-neglected training is in my opinion the most important branch of education, not only for the making of a healthy robust temperament but even more for its moral effect. I cannot say often enough that a good education ought to be negative. If the vices can be prevented from springing up virtue will be assured. This can easily be effected in a good public education. Keep the children always busy, not with boring lessons beyond their comprehension, which they hate if for nothing else than being compelled to stay in one place, but with exercises which give pleasure by satisfying the need of the growing body for movement and in other ways as well.

'At Berne a very unusual training is given to the young patricians leaving college. It is what is called the External State. This is a copy in miniature of the constituent elements of the government of the republic. There are a senate, magistrates, officers, ushers, advocates, and lawsuits, judgments and ceremonies. This State has even its own small undertakings and has some revenues. It is sanctioned and protected by the supreme government as a training ground for the statesmen who will one day direct public affairs in the same offices which in the first instance they fill only in play.

'Whatever form public education takes, it is advisable to establish a college of magistrates of the highest rank for its management. These would appoint, dismiss and change, as seems good to them, not only the principals and heads of the colleges (themselves candidates for high office) but also the games masters. Considering the fact that it is on these institutions that the hope of the republic and the future glory of the nation depends, it is surprising that nobody but myself seems to realise their importance.

'I have only given suggestions here, but these will suffice for those to whom I address myself. These ideas of mine though badly worked out show how by methods unknown to the modern world the ancients produced in men a vigour of soul, a patriotic zeal, a high regard for the essential human qualities such as are not found among us but which lie latent in every human heart only awaiting to be called into active life by the right institutions. If you direct education, usages, customs and morals in this spirit you will give this stimulus to the Polish people, and the nation will date its re-birth from the terrible crisis through which she is now passing. She will renew herself and acquire in this new age all the vigour of a young nation.'

So much for Rousseau's scheme of educational reform. But he has one more point germane to it before passing on to the discussion of the problems of government. Big nations, he has maintained consistently, are bad nations: this is 'the first and chief source of the misfortunes of the human race'.

On the other hand, almost all small states whether republics or monarchies enjoy prosperity, because their people know each other and are mutually helpful, and their rulers are able to exercise an effective supervision of their affairs. Rousseau recommends the Poles to develop a system of federal government and by doing so to secure the advantages of both large and small states.

National education, whether it be the organised kind presented in the *Encyclopédie* and in the Polish memorandum or the informal public education of Geneva, differs substantially from the individualistic scheme of the *Emile*. How deep does the difference go? Are the two just different applications of the same principles, or are they based on different and possibly conflicting principles? On any view, it must be remembered, education is double-sided: it can be thought of as the preparation which the individual needs for social life, or again as the personal upgrowing of this social being. According to one's political philosophy or the requirements of the particular situation calling for action, the emphasis is likely to be on the one side or the other; but on any adequate formulation of the educational aim both considerations must have a place. There is no inevitable inconsistency in planning a method of education for a particular child who is being brought up under the domestic conditions of an aristocratic family (as in the *Emile*), and planning a method that will make all children good citizens of their community (as in the Polish setting). Is there in fact any considerable difference in the ultimate outcomes of the two ways of education advocated by Rousseau? Will Emile not be an unsatisfactory member of society? Will the Polish citizen not be an unsatisfactory person? Confronted with this question, Rousseau would certainly have maintained that there was no fundamental contradiction in his different proposals: that what contradiction there is arises in the attempt to fit a child for a society which does not allow him to live his own proper life and that in a good society the difficulty would not exist. In the *Emile*, he is thinking of children growing up in France or one of the other great states, so big that (according to him) there can be no personal loyalty to the state and therefore no scope for individual personality. From this he deduces the need for a choice on the educator's part between making a man and making a citizen, and he opts for the man. In the New Education for Poland, he assumes a transformed Poland, broken up into a confederation of small states with rulers as wise and as devoted as Plato's Guardians; and the training he recommends is for national service, with scarcely a thought for the children as children or as individuals. It is true that when Emile becomes a man he gets smuggled back into the social system as a benevolent feudal landlord, and that when the Polish children are being drilled for citizenship their exercises are described as negative education. But in effect the two educational ideals never come together and never can come together. If the nation-states are as bad as Rousseau depicts them, the natural man of his making can never possibly become a citizen: if his ideal-states created by the indoctrination of the young are as good as he thinks them, they have no room in them for real persons with powers of responsible choice.

What is the moral? That like all the educators and philosophers who have been inspired to fresh thought and endeavour by the *Emile* we must re-think his premises and adapt his practical recommendations to our own conditions. By the fact that Rousseau, starting from an extreme individualism, was led by the dialectic of his thinking to the other extreme of state socialism, we have the problem set for us of finding ways and means of reconciling the opposites in theory and practice. Actually in the two centuries since the *Emile* was written, the nations of Europe have made some considerable progress in this direction. In spite of all the confusions which the intensification of nationalism has caused in the various countries, there are few now in any country who would take the pessimistic view of society which Rousseau took. It is just not true that ordinary people have no proper life of their own, even in the big states. Democratic procedures, popular education, newspapers and broadcasting, have combined to make possible an educative citizenship, and size of area and population is no longer a serious obstacle to effective membership of city or nation, as it was in the eighteenth century. Even our Utopias have undergone a radical change. It is true that the faith in compulsive state action to bring about better conditions of life is dangerously strong, and that large-scale indoctrination in despite of individual rights to freedom of thought prevails, even outside the dictator countries. But the welfare state of today with all its limitations is concerned with individual well-being; and scientific thinking under the conditions of democratic life goes some considerable way to ensure the freedom of thought which is necessary for good personality. The antithesis between Nature and Society which Rousseau with some justification took for granted is less deep than it once was, and the problem it presents is less hopeless.

Behind the political issues involved in the relation of individual and community there is a philosophical question of great moment. Rousseau's contradictions come from conflicting ideas about human life, which for him were largely in the region of intuition. The dominating idea in the *Emile* is that of the personal value of the individual, probably derived by him (unconsciously) from the Calvinistic theology of Geneva. 'Man,' he says in *La Nouvelle Héloïse*, written about the same time as the *Emile*, 'is too noble a being to be obliged to serve as a mere instrument for others, and should not be employed at what he is fit for, without also taking into account what is fit for him: for men are not made for their stations, but their stations for men.' Man, in short, should always be treated as an end in and to himself (to use the language of Kant) and never as a mere means either to the state or to other men. The difficulty about this conception of man is to get any kind of community on these terms. How can any enduring co-operation be achieved by individuals making such a large claim of rights? When Rousseau comes to deal with education from the political side, the postulate of the personal worth of the individual largely disappears. His main concern is then with the well-being of the community, which he personifies as the great Whole with a continuing tradition, bound together by common feeling and directing its members by the exercise of a General Will. These members as individuals have particular wills of their own with no obvious relation to the central will, until by some form of national education their individuality is overcome and they are made subject to it. In the ideal state of Rousseau's imagining, happiness comes to the citizens, not through the satisfactions of personal desire, but from the conformity which leads them to desire what the state desires.

There is truth in both points of view. Education must make good men: education must make good citizens. Rousseau's mistake was to stop at *either-or*: either education for individuality, or education for community. It is quite true that personal aims and social aims often clash: either because the individual rebels actively or passively against social requirements and ideals, or because he is reaching beyond the existing conventions to a higher morality which his contemporaries do not understand or appreciate. When this happens on a big scale and the times seem all out of joint, the idealist is tempted to find it beyond his power to do anything to put things right, and his thoughts go back to the simplicity of a golden age or forward to some Utopia. Rousseau took both of these courses, with the result (as we have seen) that he left his problem with two solutions to a contrary effect. For a deeper idealism than his, contradictions in which a good case can be made for both sides are a challenge to fresh effort in thought or action. Every man an end to himself: the state the supreme social end. Yes, accept both propositions, but go on to ask whether it may not be possible to have a state in which the individual men with their diverse ways of life make an even better contribution to the common good than they would if they all thought and acted in the same way. This actually is the kind of answer to the difficulties of adjustment met when human beings live together, which we are now trying to work out in the democratic state. The assumption of democracy is that every citizen must find satisfaction in his own way of life, and that the better these citizens make themselves the better the state will be. From this follows a wider and wiser conception of education than was possible for Rousseau and his contemporaries, however far-seeing they might be. We recognise now that education up to the limits of personal ability and interest is an essential condition of good citizenship, and that therefore there must be an adequate provision of schooling and cultural opportunities for the whole population. In this universal education we seek to combine as best we can the development of individual capacity on a liberal basis with the civic and technical training needed to make every one efficient as worker and social being. In short we are doing our imperfect best to make every individual both man and citizen; and in spite of shortcomings we are achieving enough success in a difficult task to encourage us to persevere in the expansion and perfecting of the new education which had its beginnings with Rousseau.